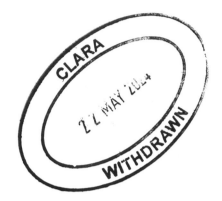

I dedicate this book to my wonderful wife Amelda…and our soon to be extended family!

Published in 2011 by:
The Irish Farmers Journal

Irish Farm Centre, Bluebell, Dublin 12
01-4199500 | www.farmersjournal.ie

© Irish Farmers Journal / Neven Maguire 2011
©Photographs: Irish Farmers Journal 2011

ISBN: 978-0-9534902-4-0

Irish Farmers Journal & Irish Country Living: Mairead Lavery, David Leydon,
Ciara O'Kelly, Jack Caffrey, Owen McGauley

Design: Márla.ie, Waterford
Editing: Orla Broderick
Print: Johnswood Press, Dublin
Photography: Jack Caffrey, Irish Farmers Journal
Food Stylist: Sharon Hearne-Smith

Foreword from Neven Maguire

It seems like only yesterday since we sent *Neven's Country Living Cookery Book Volume One* to print! The book was such a success, we felt it only right to give our loyal fans a new cookbook, which I hope you will enjoy greatly.

This book captures a selection of my most popular recipes showcased in the *Farmers Journal* magazine, *Irish Country Living* every Thursday – from simple starters, family lunches to delectable desserts, there is something for everyone to enjoy.

I'm delighted to say that my relationship with the *Farmers Journal* continues to go from strength to strength. Throughout 2011, we worked together on a number of very interesting projects, including the Ploughing Championships and the Women in Agriculture conference. Its fantastic to see so many women getting involved in agriculture now – these women are surely giving us men a run for our money!

Stay in touch with me during the year on my website **www.nevenmaguire.com**; we update recipes and information on a regular basis, and enjoy getting feedback and comments from you. You can also stay in touch with me on Facebook and Twitter.

I do hope you enjoy using this cookbook; I certainly enjoyed compiling it. Savour every moment spent in your kitchen with friends and family – it is what cooking is all about after all!

Neven

Neven Maguire
Chef & Proprietor
MacNean House & Restaurant

Foreword from Farmers Journal

Since the launch of *Neven's Country Living Cookery Book Volume One* a year ago I've had the pleasure of treating my family and friends to many of his delicious recipes. Each time I've found them easy to follow, simple to make and they've turned out just perfectly. So I'm really looking forward to trying my hand at some of the scrumptious recipes included in this – Neven's second cookery book with Irish Country Living.

Neven has been writing with Irish Country Living for over three years now and to say he is very popular with our readers would be an understatement. You just have to be on the Farmer's Journal stand at the National Ploughing Championships to see how the huge crowds get involved at his cookery demonstrations.

His spun sugar tricks are great fun for everyone and even though I've seen him weave the magic many times, it still makes me laugh. I don't think I've met anyone who works as hard as Neven or who is as nice to deal with. He is one of our greatest ambassadors for Irish food both at home and abroad – well attested to in his recent and up-coming television series.

He is also a great supporter of our farmers, artisan food producers and craft butchers, displaying the names of all his suppliers at MacNeans – his wonderful restaurant in Blacklion, Co Cavan.

Nothing is too much for him and this year as patron of Bóthar he was hugely involved in promoting the work of this aid agency leading to the donation of 143 in-calf heifers by Irish farmers to struggling families in Rwanda.

Every week I look forward to Neven's latest recipes for Irish Country Living and I know our readers do too. Now, with this book we have over 100 of these scrumptious recipes collected together under the one cover. This really is your book of essentials, an old favourite to always have in the kitchen so you can turn your hand to it year after year. A great reliable béchamel sauce, a family shepherd's pie, a good old fashioned apple tart and a pot of mixed berry jam. These winter warmers, comfort eats and classic favourites are all here for you to enjoy. I've no doubt that like *Neven's Country Living Cookery Book*, this too will become a mainstay in kitchens where good food is prepared, eaten and enjoyed.

Mairead Lavery
Editor, Irish Country Living

Irish Country Living, Ireland's favourite country magazine, is free with the Irish Farmers Journal every Thursday.

Contents

Starters and Soups

Roasted Stuffed Aubergines topped with Goat's Cheese and Cherry Tomatoes

This aubergine dish is a light tasty starter. You could also try it as a light lunch, and it is a great accompaniment to lamb. There are three excellent Irish goat's cheeses that I use: Ryefield from Fermanagh; Gortnamona from Tipperary; and Corleggy, which is made in Cavan. All three are mild and are perfect to use in this dish.

Ingredients (Serves 4)

- 2 large aubergines
- 3 tbsp rapeseed oil
- 1 red pepper
- 1 shallot, finely chopped
- small handful fresh basil leaves, shredded
- 225g (8oz) cherry tomatoes, halved
- 2 x 100g (4oz) individual goat's cheeses (rind on), thinly sliced
- Maldon sea salt and freshly ground black pepper
- lightly dressed green salad, to serve

Method

Preheat the oven to 200°C (400°F), Gas mark 6. Cut the aubergines in half and trim off the stalks. Brush the cut sides with a little of the oil and season to taste. Then place in a baking tin with the red pepper and bake for 30-35 minutes or until the flesh of the aubergine is tender and the skin of the red pepper is blackened and blistered.

Meanwhile, heat a tablespoon of the oil in a frying pan and sauté the shallot for 2-3 minutes until softened but not coloured. Set aside. Remove the vegetables from the oven and once the red pepper is cool, peel away the skin and finely chop the flesh, discarding the seeds. Place in a bowl.

Scoop out the flesh from the aubergine to within 1cm (½in) of the skin and finely chop. Add to the red pepper with the sautéed shallot and basil and season generously. Pile the red pepper mixture back into the aubergine shells and arrange the cherry tomatoes and slices of goat's cheese on top. Drizzle over the remaining oil and return to the oven for 20-25 minutes until the cherry tomatoes are lightly charred and the goat's cheese is bubbling. Arrange on serving plates with the lightly dressed green salad to serve.

Chorizo and New Potato Tortilla

I always enjoy the taste of chorizo. It is a traditional Spanish sausage, reddish in colour due to it being made with smoked paprika, which gives it that spicy taste. It is also used a lot in paella and is not as hot as chilli but a lovely tasty mouth-warmer. This recipe is a variation on the original Spanish tortilla and is perfect for brunch. Once it has cooked it should be golden brown on the outside but still succulent and moist in the middle. Sometimes I use red onions, which are that bit sweeter and I like the contrasting taste of a salad with this meal.

Ingredients (Serves 4)

- 3 tbsp rapeseed oil
- 1 large onion, thinly sliced
- 225g (8oz) new potatoes, scrubbed
- 175g (6oz) raw chorizo, peeled and diced
- 6 eggs
- Maldon sea salt and freshly ground black pepper
- lightly dressed green salad, to serve

Method

Heat two tablespoons of the oil in a non-stick frying pan with a base that is 17cm (6½in) in diameter. Add the onion and sauté for about 5 minutes until softened but not coloured. Thinly slice the potatoes into 0.5cm (¼in) slices.

Dry the sliced potatoes in a clean tea towel and add to the pan, tossing to combine. Season generously, reduce the heat and cover with a lid or flat plate, then cook gently for 10-15 minutes until almost tender. Turn them over once or twice and shake the pan occasionally to ensure they cook evenly.

Add the chorizo to the pan and cook for another 5 minutes or so until the potatoes are tender and the chorizo is sizzling and its colour has begun to bleed into the potatoes.

Break the eggs into a large bowl and add a good pinch of seasoning, then whisk lightly with a fork. When the potato and chorizo mixture is cooked, drain off any excess oil and then quickly stir into the bowl with the beaten eggs.

Wipe out the pan and use to heat the remaining tablespoon of oil. Tip in the potato and egg mixture, pressing it down gently and reduce to the lowest setting. Cook for 15-20 minutes until there is virtually no raw egg mixture left on top of the tortilla.

Invert the tortilla on to a plate, then slide back in and cook for another 5 minutes. Turn off the heat and set aside for 5 minutes to finish cooking. It should be cooked through but still moist in the centre. To serve warm or cold, turn the tortilla on to a chopping board and cut into four wedges. Place a wedge on each serving plate with a small mound of salad and serve at once.

Roast Vegetable Salad with Feta and Olives

This roasted vegetable salad makes a perfect starter or lunch with some crusty bread. Alternatively try serving it with a burger or to accompany a barbecue. You could use a sherry vinegar instead of balsamic.

Ingredients (Serves 4)

- 2 aubergines, cut into 1cm (½in) thick slices lengthways
- 2 red peppers, halved and seeded
- 6 garlic cloves, not peeled
- 3 tbsp rapeseed oil
- 2 tbsp balsamic vinegar
- 4 spring onions, finely sliced
- 8-10 pitted black olives
- large handful fresh basil leaves, shredded
- 200g (7oz) feta cheese
- Maldon sea salt and freshly ground black pepper
- crusty bread, to serve

Method

Preheat the oven to 200°C (400°F), Gas mark 6. Toss the aubergine slices, red pepper halves, garlic cloves and two tablespoons of the oil together on a baking sheet. Season well and roast for 20-25 minutes until tender.

Meanwhile, whisk the balsamic vinegar with the remaining tablespoon of oil in a large bowl.

Remove the skin from the pepper and cut into strips and roughly chop the aubergine and squeeze the garlic from their skins. Toss into the dressing with any roasting juices along with the spring onions, olives and basil. Season to taste.

Arrange the roasted vegetable salad on a large platter or individual serving plates. Crumble over the feta cheese and serve at once with a separate basket of crusty bread.

Smoked Chicken Salad with Sesame Ginger Dressing and Crispy Vegetables

I love to serve this as a starter with lots of crusty bread and wonderful Irish butter. A great supplier of smoked chicken is Ummera smoked products from Timoleague in West Cork. Smoked chicken is also excellent in sandwiches or with pasta so it's well worth seeking out.

Ingredients (Serves 4)

- sunflower oil, for deep frying
- 1 large carrot, peeled
- 1 courgette
- 2 smoked chicken breasts
- 25g (1oz) baby salad leaves

For the Dressing:
- 1 tsp finely grated root ginger
- 2 tbsp white wine vinegar
- 1 tbsp dark soy sauce
- 2 tbsp rapeseed oil
- 2 tbsp toasted sesame oil
- Maldon sea salt and freshly ground black pepper

Method

Heat a deep-fat fryer filled with sunflower oil to 170°C (340°F). Shave the carrot and courgette into thin strips or ribbons, using a potato peeler or mandolin. Blanch the strips in a large pan of boiling salted water for 1 minute until just tender but still with a little bite. Remove with a slotted spoon and drain well on kitchen paper.

Working in batches, deep-fry the vegetable strips for about 30 seconds to 1 minute until crisp and golden brown. Drain well on kitchen paper.

Meanwhile, make the dressing. Place the ginger in a small bowl with the white wine vinegar and soy sauce. Stir until well combined and then slowly whisk in the oil and sesame oils to emulsify and thicken. Season to taste.

Thinly slice the smoked chicken breasts, discarding the skin and arrange in the centre of each serving plate. Pile a small amount of the salad leaves in the centre of the chicken, then arrange the crisp vegetable ribbons around the outside of the plate. Spoon over the dressing to serve.

Smoked Salmon and Avocado Salad

For a tasty starter, it is hard to beat smoked salmon, and do make sure you buy good-quality smoked salmon for this dish. It is worth it. This tasty starter looks so appetising on the plate. I always enjoy it and it literally takes minutes to make.

Ingredients (Serves 2)

- 2 eggs
- 150g (5oz) smoked salmon slices
- 4 tbsp rapeseed oil
- juice of 1 lemon
- few handfuls of mixed salad leaves
- 1 firm ripe avocado
- 6 cherry tomatoes, halved or quartered
- 1 tbsp snipped fresh chives
- Maldon sea salt and freshly ground black pepper
- brown wheaten bread, to serve (see Baking page 168)

Method

Place the eggs in a pan of cold water and bring to the boil, then reduce the heat and simmer for 8-10 minutes until hard-boiled. Remove from the water with a slotted spoon and run under cold water to cool them down quickly. Crack off the shells and cut each hard-boiled egg into quarters.

Arrange the smoked salmon flat on serving plates, leaving a small hole in the centre. Quickly make the dressing in a bowl by whisking the oil and lemon juice together with some seasoning. Toss the salad leaves in half of the dressing and arrange them in the centre of each serving plate.

Cut the avocado in half and remove the stone, then peel and cut into slices. Arrange the pieces of hard-boiled egg, avocado and cherry tomatoes over and around the leaves and drizzle the remaining dressing on top. Scatter over the chives and serve immediately with the brown wheaten bread.

Parma Ham and Rocket Rolls

Rocket is a peppery salad leaf. I get mine from Rod Alston at the Organic Centre in Rossinver. He was telling me that rocket is one of the most viable varieties for gardeners to grow here. These Parma ham and rocket rolls can be made well in advance and kept in the fridge until you are ready to use them. When cutting the Parma, don't worry if each slice is not perfect. You can neaten them up as you roll them.

Ingredients (Serves 6-8)

- 150g (5oz) ricotta cheese
- 2 tbsp basil pesto (see Essentials page 193)
- 10 slices Parma ham
- 50g (2oz) wild rocket, tough stalks removed
- Maldon sea salt and freshly ground black pepper

Method

Mix the ricotta cheese with the pesto in a small bowl and season generously. Carefully cut each slice of Parma ham in half across the width and arrange on a clean work surface.

Spread a heaped teaspoon of the ricotta mixture in a thin, even layer over each piece of Parma ham and then lay a few sprigs of rocket lengthways across each slice, leaving the sprig ends poking out of the top. Roll up each one and arrange five on each serving plate. Cover loosely with clingfilm until you are ready to serve them.

Warm Potato Pancake with Mushrooms and Crème Fraîche

This is a suitable recipe for a vegetarian and also makes delicious use of leftover potatoes. It makes a nice starter, and the crème fraîche lightens the whole dish.

Ingredients (Serves 4)

For the potato pancakes:
- 2 eggs
- 125g (4½oz) self-raising flour
- 75g (3oz) cooked mashed potato (leftovers are fine)
- 225ml (8floz) milk
- 2 tbsp chopped fresh mixed herbs (such as parsley and chives)
- 2 spring onions finely chopped
- sunflower oil, for frying

Mushroom and Leek Topping:
- 50g (2oz) butter
- 100g (4oz) mixed mushrooms, sliced (such as chestnut, shiitake and button)
- 2 baby leeks, trimmed and thinly sliced
- 1 bunch spring onions, trimmed and thinly sliced
- Maldon sea salt and freshly ground black pepper
- creme fraîche, to serve

Method

Preheat the oven to 180°C (350°F), Gas mark 4 and put in a large non-stick baking sheet to heat up. To make the pancakes, sieve the flour and a pinch of salt into a bowl. Make a well in the centre and break the eggs into it. Gradually pour in the milk, beating continuously. Add the cooked mashed potato with the herbs. Season to taste and mix well to form a smooth batter similar in consistency to single cream.

Heat a thin film of the oil in a large heavy-based frying pan. Ladle in a quarter of the potato pancake batter and cook over a medium heat for about 1-2 minutes on each side, then using a fish slice transfer to the baking sheet and cook for another 6-8 minutes until risen and set while you cook the remainder. Keep warm.

Meanwhile, make the mushroom and leek topping, add the butter to the pan that you've cooked the potato pancakes in and then tip in the mushrooms, leeks and spring onions. Sauté over a low heat for 5 minutes until just tender and cooked through, then season to taste. Spoon the mushroom mixture into the centre of warmed serving plates. Place a pancake on each warmed serving plate and spoon over the mushroom mixture. Add a spoonful of crème fraîche to each one to serve.

Oriental Avocado and Crab Salad

This avocado and crab with ginger dressing is a particular favourite of mine. It is colourful and tasty. Sweet chilli sauce is so versatile, so I use it in lots of dishes, and the ginger adds a great kick to this dressing.

Ingredients (Serves 4)

- 250g (9oz) fine rice noodles
- 1 firm ripe avocado
- 250g (9oz) fresh cooked white crabmeat
- 1 red onion, very finely sliced
- 1 tbsp chopped fresh coriander
- juice of 1 lime
- 1 yellow pepper, halved, seeded and diced

For the Dressing:
- 3 tbsp sweet chilli sauce (Thai Gold)
- 1cm (½in) piece root ginger, peeled and grated
- 1 tbsp balsamic vinegar
- salt and freshly ground black pepper

Method

To make the ginger dressing, place the sweet chilli sauce in a bowl with the ginger and balsamic vinegar and two tablespoons of water. Whisk together until well combined. Set aside until needed.

To make the crab salad, soak the rice noodles in a bowl of very hot water for 5 minutes until soft or cook according to packet instructions or until soft. Drain and set aside to cool.

Cut the avocado in half and remove the stone, then peel and cut the flesh into bite-sized pieces. Place in a bowl with the crabmeat, red onion, coriander, lime juice and yellow pepper. Season to taste and then using a large fork, fold everything together until nicely combined. Arrange on serving plates and drizzle over the dressing to serve.

Sticky Lemon Chicken Wings

Children love these baked chicken wings. They are just so easy to make and taste absolutely delicious. If you have any leftover, leave them to cool down and chill in a plastic container, then take them on a picnic or put into a lunchbox for school. Get good quality chicken wings, free range or organic are best. Alternatively you could use drumsticks or thighs which are just as good.

Ingredients (Serves 4-6)

- 12 large chicken wings
- 25g (1oz) butter
- finely grated rind and juice of 1 lemon
- 2 tbsp dark soy sauce
- 1 tbsp clear honey
- 2 tbsp sweet chilli sauce (Thai Gold)
- Maldon sea salt and freshly ground black pepper
- jacket potatoes and corn on the cob, to serve

Method

Preheat oven to 200°C (400°F), Gas mark 6. Using a strong pair of scissors, snip the tip off each chicken wing and discard.

Melt the butter in a bowl in the microwave or in a small pan. Stir in the lemon rind and juice with the soy sauce, honey and sweet chilli sauce. Season to taste.

Arrange the chicken wings on a rack set over a baking tin and brush both sides of the wings with the lemon butter mixture. Roast for 30-40 minutes, turning and basting once or twice with the remaining lemon butter mixture until cooked through and golden brown. Arrange on warmed serving plates with jacket potatoes and corn on the cob to serve.

Smoked Bacon and Garlic Mushroom Vol-Au-Vents

This is a great recipe to do if you want to be organised well in advance. And take note that the smoked bacon and garlic mushrooms also make a great pasta sauce. By the way, if you don't have the vol-au-vents, you could just serve it on toast.

Ingredients (Serves 6)

- 1 tbsp rapeseed oil
- 1 small onion, diced
- 1 large garlic clove, crushed
- 100g (4oz) smoked bacon, rind removed and diced
- 225g (8oz) button mushrooms, quartered
- 300ml (¼ pint) milk
- 150ml (¼ pint) cream
- 2 tsp cornflour
- 6 large vol-au-vent cases, thawed
- lightly dressed mixed green salad, to serve

Method

Preheat the oven to 200°C (400°F), Gas mark 6. Heat a heavy-based frying pan. Add the oil and fry the onion, garlic and smoked bacon for 4-5 minutes until the onion is soft and the smoked bacon has begun to crisp up. Add the mushrooms and mix well to combine. Cook for another 6-8 minutes until the mushrooms are cooked through and tender.

Add the milk to the mushroom mixture with the cream and bring to a simmer. Mix two tablespoons of water with the cornflour in a small dish and then add to the sauce to make it thicken. Bring back to a simmer, stirring continuously, then reduce heat and simmer for about 5 minutes to allow the flavours to mingle. Remove from the heat and season to taste.

Meanwhile, arrange the vol-au-vent cases on a non-stick baking sheet and cook for 10-15 minutes or according to packet instructions. Just as the cases are cooked, reheat the smoked bacon and mushroom mixture. Arrange the hot vol-au-vent cases on serving plates and carefully remove the lids. Add a little salad to the side of each one, then spoon in the smoked bacon and mushroom filling and top with the lids to serve.

Parsnip and Honey Soup

We have such good honey in Ireland. I have been using Mileeven a lot, which is made in Piltown, Co. Kilkenny. Parsnips are great simply roasted with honey as it compliments their natural sweetness. I like to garnish this soup with some crunchy croutons which can be done in a little oil on a heavy-based frying pan or in the oven.

Ingredients (Serves 6-8)

- 50g (2oz) butter
- 1 large onion, chopped
- 8 parsnips, chopped
- 1 tsp chopped fresh thyme
- 2 tbsp clear honey
- 1.75 litres (3 pints) vegetable or chicken stock (see Essentials page 213 and page 215)
- 100ml (3½fl oz) cream
- Maldon sea salt and freshly ground black pepper
- croutons, to garnish

Method

Melt the butter in a large pan and cook the onion for a few minutes until softened but not coloured. Stir in the parsnips and thyme, then season to taste. Cook for a few minutes and then stir in the honey and cook for another 5 minutes until lightly golden and caramelised, stirring occasionally.

Pour the stock into the pan and bring to the boil, then reduce the heat and simmer for about 30 minutes until the parsnips are completely tender and the liquid has slightly reduced. Stir in the cream and allow to heat through.

Purée the soup in batches in a food processor or liquidiser until smooth, then pour back into a clean pan; or use a hand blender leaving the soup in the pan. Season to taste and reheat gently. Ladle the soup into warmed serving bowls and garnish with croutons and a good grinding of black pepper to serve.

Roasted Red Pepper and Tomato Soup

Chargrilled peppers have the most wonderful, smoky sweetness, which I just adore. Collect as much of the juice as possible as you peel them, as it really has a great flavour. In the restaurant I don't use any flour in my soups these days. I was always conscious of our diners who were coeliac, and have now come to prefer soups without flour and it helps keep them so much lighter too.

Ingredients (Serves 4-6)

- 4 red peppers, halved, cored and seeded
- 2 tomatoes, quartered
- 5 tbsp rapeseed oil
- 1 tbsp balsamic vinegar
- ½ tsp chopped fresh thyme
- 2 onions, finely chopped
- 2 garlic cloves, crushed
- 2 tbsp tomato purée
- 1.2 litres (2 pints) vegetable or chicken stock (see Essentials page 213 and 215)
- 2 tbsp torn fresh basil
- Maldon sea salt and freshly ground black pepper
- basil pesto, to garnish see Essentials page 193)
- freshly baked ciabatta, to serve (optional)

Method

Preheat oven to 190°C (375°F), Gas mark 5. Arrange the pepper halves and tomatoes in a baking tin, cut side up. Drizzle over four tablespoons of the oil and then sprinkle the vinegar, thyme and a teaspoon of the salt on top. Place in the oven and roast for 30-40 minutes or until softened and lightly golden.

When the peppers are cold enough to handle, slip the skins off the peppers and discard, then chop roughly the flesh, reserving as much of the juice as possible. Set aside with tomatoes until needed.

Heat the remaining tablespoon of oil in a pan, add the onions and garlic and sweat for 2-3 minutes until lightly golden, stirring occasionally. Add the reserved pepper flesh, tomatoes with the tomato purée and stock and bring to the boil. Reduce the heat and simmer for 10-15 minutes until slightly reduced. Add the basil or pesto and then blitz with a hand blender until smooth or use a food processor.

Season to taste. To serve, ladle the soup into warmed serving bowls and drizzle with a little basil pesto, then serve with some ciabatta bread on the side, if liked.

Leek and Potato Soup with Smoked Bacon

My mum used to make this leek and potato soup with smoked bacon all the time when we were young. It can also be served chilled but I prefer it piping hot and served with a chunk of homemade bread. I reserve some of the cooked potato cubes to give the finished soup texture, but if you decide to prepare it in advance these will need to be reheated in the microwave or in a small pan. Use a tiny knob of butter to prevent them from sticking until heated through.

Ingredients (Serves 6-8)

- 8 rindless smoked streaky bacon rashers
- 50g (2oz) butter
- 450g (1lb) leeks, trimmed and roughly chopped
- 1 onion, roughly chopped (about 225g (8oz) in total)
- 1 potato, cut into cubes (about 225g (8oz) in total)
- 25g (1oz) plain flour
- 1.75 litres (3 pints) chicken stock (see Essentials page 215)
- 200ml (7fl oz) cream
- 12 fresh basil leaves, plus extra to garnish
- Maldon sea salt and freshly ground black pepper

Method

Preheat the grill to medium. Cut four of the bacon rashers in half and arrange them on the grill rack. Cook for 3-4 minutes on each side until crisp and golden. Transfer to a plate and set aside to use as a garnish.

Dice the remaining four rashers. Melt the butter in a large pan and gently fry the diced bacon with the leeks and onion over a low heat for about 5 minutes until softened but not coloured. Add the potato and flour, stirring well to combine and then cook for another 2 minutes, stirring. Gradually add the stock, stirring to prevent any lumps forming. Bring to the boil, then reduce the heat and simmer for 15 minutes or until the potatoes are completely tender, stirring occasionally to prevent the mixture sticking to the bottom of the pan.

Add 150ml (¼ pint) of the cream to the soup and simmer for another 5 minutes, stirring occasionally. Add the basil and season to taste. Remove from the heat and reserve a large spoonful of potato cubes to use as garnish. Purée the soup in batches in a food processor or liquidiser until smooth, then pour back into a clean pan; or use a hand blender leaving the soup in the pan. Reheat gently for a few minutes, stirring occasionally. Place the remaining 50ml (2fl oz) of the cream in a bowl and lightly whip.

To serve, divide the reserved hot potato cubes between warmed serving bowls. Ladle over the hot soup and drizzle the whipped cream on top. Garnish with the crispy bacon rashers and some basil leaves to serve.

Carrot, Ginger and Honey Soup

This carrot, ginger and honey soup is easy to make and actually does not need any stock, which is a major bonus. It also has the most fantastic vibrant colour and costs little or nothing to make. What more could you want?

Ingredients (Serves 6-8)

- 75g (3oz) butter
- 1 onion, thinly sliced
- 20g (¾oz) root ginger, peeled and finely chopped
- 675g (1½lb) carrots, grated
- 1 tbsp clear honey
- 1 tsp fresh lemon juice
- 900ml (1½ pints) boiling water
- Maldon sea salt and freshly ground white pepper
- lightly whipped cream and snipped fresh chives, to garnish

Method

Melt the butter in a large pan. Add the onion and ginger, then cook gently for 2-3 minutes until softened but not coloured, stirring occasionally. Add in the carrots, honey and lemon juice. Pour the boiling water into the carrot mixture and bring to the boil. Reduce the heat and simmer for 45 minutes until slightly reduced and the carrots are tender.

Remove the soup from the heat and blitz with a hand blender until smooth or use a food processor. Season to taste and reheat gently, then ladle into warmed serving bowls. Drizzle a little cream into each serving and garnish down the middle with a thin line of chives to serve.

Pea and Mint Soup

This pea and mint soup is delicious and light. It is so refreshing and you can also serve it chilled if you like. It is a particular favourite of my mother. She wasn't well recently and this was one of the things she loved to give her a lift. You could use courgettes instead of peas if you like. It is a great way to use them up if you have grown a lot of them.

Ingredients (Serves 4-6)

- 1 bunch spring onions, trimmed and roughly chopped
- 1 medium potato, diced
- 1 garlic clove, crushed
- 900ml (1 ½ pints) vegetable or chicken stock (see Essentials page 213 and page 215)
- 250g (9oz) frozen peas
- 4 tbsp chopped fresh mint, plus extra sprigs to garnish
- large pinch caster sugar
- 1 tbsp fresh lemon or lime juice
- 150ml (¼ pint) cream
- Maldon sea salt and freshly ground black pepper
- crusty bread, to serve

Method

Put the spring onions into a large pan with the potato, garlic and stock. Bring to the boil, then turn down the heat and simmer for 15 minutes or until the potato is very soft, stirring occasionally.

Add the peas to the soup base and simmer for 10 minutes and not any longer or you will lose the lovely fresh flavour of the peas. Stir in the mint, sugar and lemon or lime juice and then leave to cool slightly.

Pour the pea mixture into a food processor or liquidiser and whizz until as smooth as you like or use a hand blender leaving the soup in the pan. Stir in the cream and season to taste. To serve the soup cold, cool it down quickly by placing it in a bowl set on top of ice, then chill in the fridge until ice cold - you may need to add more stock to the soup before serving as it will thicken as it cools.

To serve hot, return the soup to a simmer, stirring until heated through. Ladle the soup into serving bowls, and garnish with the reserved peas and fresh mint sprigs. Have a basket of crusty bread to hand around separately.

Lamb, Beef and Game

Grilled Rib-Eye Steak with Smoked Paprika and Red Pepper Butter

These days I hear there is less fillet and striploin being sold and rib-eye has become more popular. It is good value. I always bring steaks to room temperature by removing them from the fridge 30 minutes before I want to cook them. This butter will complement any grilled meat or try stirring it into some pasta. It will keep in the fridge for 2 days or can be frozen.

Ingredients (Serves 4)

- 4 x 225g (8oz) dry aged rib-eye steaks
- 100ml (3 ½fl oz) rapeseed oil
- 2 garlic cloves, crushed
- 1 tsp chopped fresh thyme

For the Butter:
- 1 small red pepper
- 175g (6oz) butter
- ½ tsp chopped fresh thyme
- 1 tsp chopped fresh flat-leaf parsley
- 1 tsp smoked paprika
- 1 tbsp cream
- Maldon sea salt and freshly ground black pepper
- baked potatoes and lightly dressed mixed green salad, to serve

Method

To make the flavoured butter, preheat the grill. Place the pepper on the grill rack and cook for 20-25 minutes until the skin is blackened and blistered, turning regularly. Transfer to a bowl and cover with clingfilm, then leave to cool completely.

Remove the skin, core and seeds from the pepper and roughly chop the flesh, then place in a food processor. Add the butter, thyme, parsley and paprika and purée until smooth. Beat in the cream and then scrape out onto a square of parchment paper and roll into a cylinder, twisting the ends to secure. Chill for at least 4 hours – up to 24 hours is fine.

Trim the rib-eye steaks of any excess fat, place in a non-metallic dish and add the oil, garlic and thyme. Cover with clingfilm and leave in the fridge to marinate overnight.

Remove the steaks from the fridge at least half an hour before you wish to cook them, then shake off any excess marinade and season to taste. Grill, barbecue or pan-fry the steaks over a high heat for 6-7 minutes for medium rare, or to your liking. Allow to rest for 5 minutes on warmed serving plates.

Remove the flavoured butter from the fridge and remove the paper, then cut into slices. Place the butter slices on top of the grilled steaks and add a baked potato and some mixed salad to each plate to serve.

Irish Stew

I never tire of a bowl of steaming hot Irish stew, but it is the attention to detail that makes this dish one of the world's great classics. This is my version, which I have developed over the years. Some people say you shouldn't use carrots, but this began as one of my mother's recipes and I am still putting carrots in! Ask you local craft butcher for some neck or shoulder cuts. If you make it the day before and warm it up, your meat will be more tender. We serve a small portion of this stew in the restaurant in a dish featuring four versions of cooked lamb.

Ingredients (Serves 4)

- 900g (2lb) boneless lamb neck or shoulder, trimmed and cut into cubes
- 50g (2oz) pearl barley, washed
- 225g (8oz) potatoes, cut into chunks
- 225g (8oz) carrots, thickly sliced
- 225g (8oz) leeks, well trimmed and thickly sliced
- 225g (8oz) baby pearl onions, peeled
- 100g (4oz) rindless piece smoked bacon, diced
- 2 fresh thyme sprigs

For the Lamb Stock:
- 450g (1lb) lamb bones
- 1 carrot, cut into cubes
- 1 onion, sliced
- 2 whole peppercorns
- 1 bouquet garni (bundle of herbs tied together with string)
- Maldon sea salt and freshly ground black pepper
- chopped fresh parsley, to garnish
- colcannon, to serve

Method

To make the stock, place the lamb bones in a large pan with the carrot, onion, peppercorns and bouquet garni. Cover with cold water and bring to the boil, then reduce the heat and simmer gently for two hours, until you have achieved a good flavour. Leave to cool, then skim off any scum and/or fat and strain into a large jug (you should have about 1 litre (1¾ pints) of stock. Cover with clingfilm and chill until needed.

Place the boneless lamb pieces in a clean, large heavy-based pan and pour over the reserved stock. Bring to the boil, then skim off any scum from the surface and stir in the barley. Reduce the heat and simmer for 50 minutes, until slightly reduced and the lamb is almost tender. Add the potatoes to the lamb with the carrots, leeks, baby pearl onions, smoked bacon and thyme and simmer for 30 minutes, or until the lamb and vegetables are completely tender but still holding their shape. Season to taste. Transfer the stew into a warmed casserole dish and scatter over the parsley. Serve straight to the table with a separate dish of the colcannon.

Lamb Burgers with Yoghurt and Mint Dip

Lamb makes a delicious, aromatic, full-on flavour burger. Get some Quality Assured meat from your butcher. It is good value now, and your butcher will mince it for you. The natural yoghurt with mint goes very well with the full flavour of these burgers and helps cut through the richness of the meat.

Ingredients (Serves 4)

- 450g (1lb) lean lamb mince
- 1 small onion, diced
- 1 garlic clove, crushed
- 2 tbsp chopped fresh mint
- 1 tbsp chopped fresh oregano
- 1 tsp ground coriander
- 1 tbsp sweet chilli sauce (Thai Gold)
- 4 burger buns or small rolls
- good handful wild rocket leaves

For the Dip:
- ½ small cucumber, halved and seeded
- 150g (5oz) natural yoghurt
- 1 garlic clove, crushed
- 1 tbsp chopped fresh mint, plus extra leaves to serve
- squeeze of lemon juice
- Maldon sea salt and freshly ground black pepper
- 1 lemon, cut into wedges, to garnish

Method

Mix together the lamb, onion, garlic, mint, oregano, ground coriander, sweet chilli sauce and season to taste. Divide the mixture into four portions and shape into 2cm (¾in) thick burgers.

Heat a griddle pan or the barbecue and cook the lamb burgers for 10-15 minutes, turning occasionally, until cooked through and well browned. Transfer to a plate and leave to rest for a couple of minutes.

To make the dip, grate the cucumber and squeeze out excess liquid with your hands and place in a bowl. Mix in the yoghurt, garlic and mint. Add some salt and a squeeze of lemon juice. Warm the burger buns or rolls on the griddle pan or barbecue.

Serve the lamb burgers in the warm burger buns topped with the rocket, mint leaves and a good dollop of the yoghurt and mint dip. Arrange on warmed serving plates and garnish with the lemon wedges to serve.

Grilled Beef Kebabs with Lemon Couscous

These kebabs get better the longer you marinate them. They make a great family meal and couscous is a good alternative to rice. These days, I know a lot of people who serve both and have a big bowl of rice and one of couscous on the table so everyone can help themselves. Any leftover couscous is also delicious cold with a sprinkling of lemon juice.

Ingredients (Serves 4)

- 450g (1lb) sirloin steak, cut into 2.5cm (1in) cubes
- 1 tbsp sweet chilli sauce (Thai Gold)
- 1 tbsp honey
- 2 tbsp dark soy sauce
- 2 garlic cloves, crushed
- 1 tsp freshly grated root ginger
- 1 tbsp chilli oil
- 2 tomatoes, cut into wedges
- 2 tbsp chopped fresh flat-leaf parsley, plus extra to garnish

For the Couscous:
- 350g (12oz) couscous
- 6 tbsp rapeseed oil
- finely grated rind and juice of 2 lemons
- 600ml (1 pint) vegetable stock (see Essentials page 213)
- Maldon sea salt and freshly ground black pepper
- cucumber raita, to serve

Method

To marinade the beef, mix the sweet chilli sauce, honey, soy sauce, garlic, ginger and chilli oil in a shallow non-metallic dish. Add the beef, stirring to coat and then cover with clingfilm and leave at room temperature for 2 hours to allow the flavours to develop. You can also leave this to marinate overnight for an even better flavour.

Preheat a heavy-based griddle or large frying pan. Thread the marinated beef and tomato wedges onto 8 x 15cm (6in) metal or bamboo skewers. Add to the heated pan and cook over a medium heat for 12-15 minutes until cooked through, turning frequently.

To make the couscous, place it in a large bowl and add four tablespoons of the oil and the lemon juice. Mix well, ensuring that all the grains are completely coated. Heat the stock in a small pan and season generously. Pour over the couscous and allow to sit in a warm place for 6-8 minutes, until all the liquid has absorbed, stirring occasionally. Stir the remaining oil with the lemon rind into the couscous and place over a low heat for a couple of minutes to warm through, fluffing up the grains with a fork. Season to taste.

Divide the couscous among warmed serving plates and arrange two of the kebabs on top of each one. Add a dollop of the cucumber raita and garnish with a little parsley to serve.

Spicy Lamb Cutlets with Guacamole and Tomato Salsa

These lamb cutlets are delicious and cooking them under the grill keeps them wonderfully succulent. Both the guacamole and the salsa are very versatile so you will have lots of uses for these recipes. Both originate from Mexico. Avocados are full of healthy monounsaturated fats and fibre. Traditionally guacamole was made by mashing the ripe avocados with a pestle and mortar but I find a blender works very well for a smooth result.

Ingredients (Serves 4)

- 2 tbsp rapeseed oil
- 1 tsp ground cumin
- 1 tsp ground coriander
- 2 tsp paprika
- 12 lamb cutlets, well trimmed

For the Tomato Salsa:
- 1 tbsp rapeseed oil
- 1 onion, finely chopped
- 1 garlic clove, crushed
- 400g can chopped tomatoes
- 1 tbsp sweet chilli sauce (Thai Gold)
- ¼ tsp sugar
- pinch chilli powder
- 3 tbsp chopped fresh coriander

For the Guacamole:
- 2 ripe avocados
- 2 tbsp finely chopped red onion
- 2 ripe tomatoes, peeled, seeded and diced
- 1 garlic clove, crushed
- 2 tbsp chopped fresh coriander
- 1 tbsp chilli sauce
- juice of 1 lime

- Maldon sea salt and freshly ground black pepper
- fresh coriander leaves, to garnish

Method

First make the tomato salsa. Heat the oil in a pan and sauté the onion and garlic for a couple of minutes until softened. Add the tomatoes and chilli sauce along with the sugar and chilli powder. Stir to combine and then simmer for 10-15 minutes until well reduced and thickened, stirring occasionally. Leave to cool, then stir in the coriander and season to taste. Transfer to a serving bowl.

Preheat the grill to medium. Mix the oil in a shallow dish with the cumin, coriander and paprika and season to taste. Add the lamb cutlets, turning to coat and leave at room temperature for 15 minutes to allow the flavours to penetrate the meat (or up to 24 hours covered with clingfilm in the fridge is fine).

Remove the lamb cutlets from the dish, shaking off any excess oil and arrange on a grill rack. Place under the preheated grill and cook for 4-5 minutes on each side until cooked through and tender.

Meanwhile, make the guacamole, cut the avocados in half and remove the stone, then scoop out the flesh into a blender. Blend until smooth and then transfer to a bowl. Add the red onion, tomatoes, garlic, coriander, chilli sauce and lime juice. Mix until well combined and season to taste. Transfer to a serving bowl. Arrange the spicy lamb cutlets on warmed serving plates and garnish with the coriander leaves. Place the tomato salsa and guacamole on the table so that everyone can help themselves.

Chargrilled Beef Salad

I've discovered on my travels that the people of Thailand and neighbouring countries are very fond of this type of chargrilled salad. This is a really authentic recipe I picked up along the way and have always enjoyed cooking it with prawns since coming home. Beef fillet is one of the most expensive cuts, but it is so tender – that is what you are paying for. Believe me, it is worth it! Ask for the best quality from your local butcher. It should have a slight marbling of fat for the best flavour.

Ingredients (Serves 4)

- 1 tsp Thai fragrant rice
- 2 dried small red chillies
- 500g (1lb 2oz) thick beef fillet
- 2 tbsp toasted sesame oil
- 5 tbsp kecap manis (sweet soy sauce)
- 1 small cucumber, peeled, halved, seeded and cut into 1cm (½in) slices
- 4 red shallots, thinly sliced
- 100g (4oz) cherry tomatoes, halved
- 1 mild red chilli, seeded and thinly sliced
- handful fresh mint leaves
- handful fresh coriander leaves
- small handful fresh basil leaves, torn
- 4 spring onions, thinly sliced
- 1 tsp caster sugar
- 4 tbsp fresh lime juice
- 3 tbsp Thai fish sauce (nam pla) (preferably Thai Gold)
- 100g (4oz) mixed green salad leaves

Method

If using a charcoal barbecue, light it 30 minutes before you want to start cooking. If using a gas barbecue, light it 10 minutes beforehand. Alternatively, use a griddle or frying pan.

Heat a dry frying pan, add the rice and toast until golden, but not burnt. Grind the rice in a coffee-grinder or pound to a powder with a pestle and mortar and set aside. Reheat the frying pan and add the dried chillies. Toast until they are smokey, tossing regularly, then grind or pound to a powder. Mix in a small bowl with the rice and set aside. If using a griddle or frying pan, place over a high heat until very hot. Cook the beef fillet over medium-hot coals on the barbecue or on the pan for 10–12 minutes, until well marked on the outside and rare to medium-rare inside. Place in a non-metallic bowl and leave to rest for 10 minutes, then mix together the sesame oil and kecap manis (sweet soy sauce) and brush all over the fillet. Cover with clingfilm and leave to marinate in a cool place for two hours, turning from time to time. Place the cucumber, shallots, cherry tomatoes, fresh chilli, herbs and spring onions in a large bowl and gently toss together to combine. Cover with clingfilm and chill until needed. Dissolve the sugar in a screw-topped jar with the lime juice and fish sauce. Set aside until needed.

To serve, thinly slice the beef and return to the bowl it has been marinating in. Combine the cucumber mixture with the fish sauce dressing and ground chilli rice, then fold into the beef. Divide the salad leaves between serving plates, and pile the beef mixture high on top to serve.

Moroccan Lamb Tagine with Green Couscous

The lamb tagine may sound like a complicated dish, however it is not and can be made a day in advance. You can use either the shoulder or the rump of lamb. Both are very good value – and remember to keep an eye out for the Irish Quality mark. There is lots of flavour in the couscous. It is a great dish to experiment with and try with different herbs.

Ingredients (Serves 6-8)

- 2 tbsp paprika
- 1 tbsp ground coriander
- 1 tbsp turmeric
- 2 tsp ground cinnamon
- 2 tsp ground cumin
- 2 tsp coarse ground black pepper
- 1.5kg (3lb 5oz) lamb shoulder, well trimmed and cut into 4cm (1½in) chunks
- 4 garlic cloves, chopped
- 2.5cm (1in) piece peeled root ginger, chopped
- 3 onions, roughly chopped
- 2 tbsp rapeseed oil
- 600ml (1 pint) tomato juice
- 600ml (1 pint) chicken stock (see Essentials page 215)
- 2 tbsp clear honey
- 225g (8oz) dates, cut in half and stones removed
- 50g (2oz) toasted flaked almonds

For the Couscous:
- 350g (12oz) couscous
- 6 tbsp rapeseed oil
- juice of 2 lemons
- 600ml (1 pint) chicken stock (see Essentials page 215)

- 4 tbsp chopped fresh flat-leaf parsley and mint
- 50g (2oz) ready-to-eat dried apricots, finely chopped
- Maldon sea salt and freshly ground black pepper
- Greek-style yoghurt and fresh coriander leaves, to garnish

Method

Mix the paprika, coriander, turmeric, cinnamon, cumin and pepper together in a large bowl. Then tip half into a small bowl and set aside. Add the lamb to the large bowl and coat in the spices. Cover with clingfilm and chill overnight.

Preheat the oven to 160°C (325°F), Gas mark 3. Place the garlic, ginger and onions into a food processor and pulse until finely minced.

Heat a large heavy-based casserole dish. Add half of the oil and brown off the marinated lamb in batches. Add the remaining oil to the pan and then add the onion mixture. Cook for a few minutes until softened but not coloured. Stir in the reserved spice mixture and cook for another minute or so until well combined.

Pour the tomato juice and stock into the pan and then add the browned lamb with the honey, stirring to combine. Bring to the boil, cover, and transfer to the oven. Cook for one hour. Then stir in the dates and cook for another hour until the lamb is completely tender and the sauce has thickened and reduced. Season to taste.

To make the couscous, place it in a large bowl and add four tablespoons of the oil and the lemon juice. Mix well, ensuring that all the grains are completely coated. Heat the stock in a small pan and season generously. Pour over the couscous and allow to sit in a warm place for 6-8 minutes, until all the liquid has absorbed, stirring occasionally. To serve, stir the remaining oil with the herbs and apricots into the couscous and arrange on warmed serving plates with the tagine. Scatter over the toasted almonds and then garnish with a dollop of the Greek yoghurt and coriander leaves.

Shepherd's Pie

This Shepherd's pie must be the ultimate comfort food. It is full of goodness and can happily be made the day before. Simply cover with clingfilm and pop in the fridge until needed. It is traditionally made with minced lamb but of course you could use beef and then call it a cottage pie!

Ingredients (Serves 4)

- 2 tbsp rapeseed oil
- 2 smoked bacon rashers, rinds removed and diced
- 450g (1lb) lean minced lamb
- 1 onion, finely chopped
- 1 garlic clove, crushed
- 4 carrots, finely diced
- 2 tbsp Worcestershire sauce
- 300ml (½ pint) beef stock (see Essentials page 214)
- 1 tbsp tomato purée
- 1 tsp chopped fresh thyme
- 1 tbsp chopped fresh flat-leaf parsley
- 100g (4oz) frozen peas

For the Cheesy Mash:
- 900g (2lb) floury potatoes, cut into even-sized pieces (such as roosters)
- 100ml (3½fl oz) milk
- 25g (1oz) butter
- 50g (2oz) Cheddar cheese, grated
- Maldon sea salt and freshly ground black pepper

Method

To prepare the cheesy mash, steam the potatoes for 20-25 minutes until cooked through and tender. Drain and return to the pan, then put on the heat for a few minutes to dry out. Remove from the heat and mash well, making sure there are no lumps. Meanwhile, heat the milk in a small pan and then beat into mashed potatoes with the butter and cheese until you have achieved a smooth mash. Season to taste and set aside until needed.

Meanwhile, heat half the oil in a heavy-based pan with a lid. Add the bacon and minced lamb and sauté until lightly browned and break up any lumps with the back of a wooden spoon. Remove from the pan with a slotted spoon and set aside.

Add the rest of the oil to the heated pan and then tip in the onion and cook for a couple of minutes until softened but not coloured. Stir in the garlic and cook for 1 minute or so, then tip in the carrots and sauté for another 5 minutes until tender. Stir in the Worcestershire sauce, then add the stock, tomato purée and thyme with the cooked mince and bacon mixture. Give everything a good stir and bring to the boil. Reduce the heat, cover and simmer gently for about 30 minutes until the minced lamb is cooked through and tender. Finally stir in the parsley and peas and season to taste.

Preheat oven to 180°C (350°F), Gas mark 4. Transfer the cooked minced lamb mixture into an ovenproof dish and leave to cool slightly for 20 minutes to allow a slight skin to form. Gently spoon the cheesy mash on top, spreading it with a fork to ensure it's even. Cook for 25-30 minutes or until the cheesy mash is bubbling and golden brown. Serve straight to the table and allow everyone to help themselves.

Roast Leg of Spring Lamb with Rosemary and Garlic

This is a fantastic dish to make with a leg of lamb. The mint mash is surprisingly good with the lamb and offers an interesting contrast to the crunchy roast potatoes. Homemade mint sauce takes no time at all, simply place a good handful of chopped fresh mint in a serving dish and stir in a teaspoon of sugar. Add a couple of tablespoons of boiling water and stir until the sugar has dissolves, then stir enough white wine vinegar to taste.

Ingredients (Serves 6)

- 1.75kg (4lb) leg of lamb
- 3 garlic cloves, sliced
- 2 fresh rosemary sprigs
- 900g (2lb) potatoes, quartered
- 50g (2oz) butter
- 1 tbsp milk
- 2 tsp mint sauce (homemade or from a jar)
- Maldon sea salt and freshly ground black pepper
- roasted carrots and beetroot, to serve

Method

Preheat the oven to 200°C (400°F), Gas mark 6. Using a sharp knife, make small incisions all over the lamb and press a garlic slice and a tiny sprig of the rosemary well into each one.

Place the leg of lamb in a roasting tin. Roast for 20 minutes and reduce the oven temperature to 180°C (350°F), Gas mark 4 and roast for 1 hour and 40 minutes for a leg of lamb this size.

After an hour in the oven, so about 40 minutes before the end of the cooking time, add carrots, beetroots and half of the potatoes into the roasting tin and quickly baste in the juices. Continue to roast until the leg of lamb is tender and the vegetables are almost done.

Cook the rest of the potatoes in a pan of boiling salted water for 20-25 minutes; then drain well and add the butter and milk. Mash until creamy, then stir in the mint sauce, mix well to combine and season to taste. Keep warm.

Transfer the leg of lamb to a carving platter and cover loosely with foil, then return the carrots and potatoes to the oven to finish cooking.

Carve the lamb into slices and arrange on warmed serving plates with the roast vegetables, potatoes and mint mash.

Seared Striploin Steak with Sauce Diane and Roast Garlic Mash

Steak and mash is always a success. Sauce Diane has its origins in the late 19th Century in France. It was originally served with game, getting its name from Diana, goddess of the hunt. It is a rich sauce and has stood the test of time. Just don't count the calories on this one. I've used rapeseed oil that comes from Donegal but there is also a very good one made in Louth. I now use it all the time in my cooking and it is great to hear of more farmers growing it across the country.

Ingredients (Serves 2)

- 2 tbsp rapeseed oil
- 2 garlic cloves, crushed
- 1 teaspoon of fresh thyme leaves
- 2 x 150g (5oz) sirloin or striploin steaks

For the Roast Garlic Mash:
- 4 garlic cloves, unpeeled
- 1 tbsp rapeseed oil
- 675g (1½lb) potatoes, cut into chunks
- 2 tbsp softened butter
- 1 tbsp cream

For the Sauce Diane:
- 2 tbsp rapeseed oil
- 25g (1oz) butter
- 1 shallot, finely chopped
- 150g (5oz) button mushrooms, trimmed and sliced
- 120ml (4fl oz) brandy
- 150ml (¼ pint) white wine
- 150ml (¼ pint) beef stock (see Essentials page 214)
- 1 tbsp Worcestershire sauce
- good pinch sugar
- 150ml (¼ pint) double cream
- 1 tbsp chopped fresh flat-leaf parsley
- squeeze of fresh lemon juice
- Maldon sea salt and freshly ground black pepper

Method

Preheat oven to 180°C (350°F), Gas mark 4. Place the oil, garlic and thyme in a shallow dish and add the steaks, turning to coat. Set aside at room temperature for 20 minutes to allow the flavours to develop.

Meanwhile, make the garlic mash, place the garlic cloves on a piece of foil and drizzle with the oil. Scrunch up the foil into a purse and cook in the oven for 30 minutes. Remove from the oven and allow to cool.

To make the sauce, heat a pan and add one of the tablespoons of the oil and the butter, then swirl until the butter has melted and is foaming. Tip in the shallot and mushrooms and sauté for 4-5 minutes until tender. Pour over the brandy, then use a match or tilt up the pan to catch the flame. It will flare up for about 5-10 seconds and then subside when the alcohol flame burns off. Add the wine, stirring to combine and then simmer until reduced by half. Stir the stock into the pan with the Worcestershire sauce, sugar and cream. Bring to the boil, then reduce the heat and simmer for 20-25 minutes or until thickened to a sauce consistency which will coat the back of a wooden spoon, stirring occasionally. Stir in the parsley and lemon juice. Season to taste. Reheat gently in a pan when needed.

Meanwhile, steam the potatoes for the mash for 20-25 minutes until tender. Open the cooled foil purse and carefully squeeze the garlic cloves from their skins. Melt the butter in a pan and add cream and the roasted garlic. Tip in the potatoes and mash until smooth, then season to taste. Spoon into a piping bag with a plain nozzle. Keep warm.

Heat an ovenproof frying pan over a high heat. Season the steaks with plenty of black pepper and cook for 2 minutes on each side to seal in the juices, then transfer to the oven and cook the steak for another 5-10 minutes, turning once, depending on how rare you like your meat (5 minutes for rare, 7 for medium and 10 for well done). Transfer the cooked steak to warmed serving plates, season with salt and set aside in a warm place to rest while you assemble the dish. Pour any juices that run off the meat into your sauce for added flavour. Drizzle the sauce around the steaks and pipe the roasted garlic mash to one side to serve.

Chilli con Carne

Here I've served this Chilli con Carne with tortilla chips but it would also be delicious with baked potatoes, warm pitta breads or rice, depending on what you fancy. Ask your butcher to prepare the rump steak for you or ask him what other cuts he has that might be suitable; any braising meat is prefect for this form of cooking.

Ingredients (Serves 6)

- 2 tbsp rapeseed oil
- 675g (1½lb) rump steak, trimmed and diced into 1cm (½in) cubes
- 2 onions, finely chopped
- 1 tsp hot chilli powder
- 1 tbsp paprika
- 1 tsp ground cumin
- 1 tsp ground coriander
- 2 tbsp dark muscovado sugar
- 3 garlic cloves, crushed
- 2 x 400g cans chopped tomatoes
- 600ml (1 pint) beef stock (see Essentials page 214)
- 2 x 400g cans red kidney beans, drained and rinsed
- Maldon sea salt and freshly ground black pepper
- crème fraîche and fresh coriander leaves, to garnish
- tortilla chips, to serve

Method

Heat the oil in a large heavy-based pan until very hot. Add the oil to the pan and sauté the beef in batches for 4-5 minutes until well browned all over, tossing occasionally. Remove with a slotted spoon, leaving the fat behind in the pan each time and place on a plate. Set aside until needed.

Add the onions to the heated pan with the chilli powder, paprika, cumin, coriander and sugar. Fry very gently for 8-10 minutes until the onions are golden and well caramelised, stirring from time to time. Do not be tempted to reduce this time down as this stage is very important for flavour.

Return the browned beef to the pan with the garlic, tomatoes and stock. Season well and bring to the boil, then reduce the heat and simmer, uncovered, on a low heat for one hour. Finally, stir in the kidney beans and cook for another 20 minutes until the meat is meltingly tender. Season to taste.

Ladle the chilli con carne into warmed serving bowls set on plates and garnish with the crème fraîche and coriander. Add a handful of tortilla chips to each plate to serve.

Roast Sirloin of Irish Beef with Red Wine Gravy

I know people will be saying that a roast beef lunch isn't cheap. But when you're making a special effort, it never fails to please the family. If you follow this recipe, you'll have the roast you want, the way you want it, and you can sit back and watch the family enjoy it. I like mine medium rare with red wine gravy, which is also a great sauce with lamb or chicken.

Ingredients (Serves 6-8)

- 3 tbsp rapeseed oil
- 2kg (4½lb) strip loin of beef
- 4 shallots, halved
- 2 garlic cloves, halved
- 3 fresh thyme sprigs
- 500ml (18fl oz) red wine
- 300ml (½ pint) beef stock (see Essentials page 214)
- pinch sugar (optional)

For the Parsnip and Potato Mash:

- 450g (1lb) parsnips, cut into pieces with any tough cores removed
- 675g (1½lb) potatoes, cut into pieces
- 50ml (2fl oz) milk
- pinch freshly grated nutmeg
- 50g (2oz) butter

For the Horseradish Sauce:

- 50g (2oz) fresh horseradish root, peeled and finely grated
- 1 tsp Dijon mustard
- 1 tbsp white wine vinegar
- 1 tsp caster sugar
- 150ml (¼ pint) whipping cream
- 2 tbsp snipped fresh chives
- Maldon sea salt and freshly ground black pepper
- steamed long stem broccoli, to serve

Method

Preheat the oven to 190°C (375°F), Gas mark 5. Heat the oil in a roasting tin and place the seasoned beef in it. Seal the meat on both sides. Cover the joint loosely with foil and put in the oven for 15 minutes per 450g (1lb) if you like your beef medium-rare. For a medium meat, cook for 15 minutes longer and a further 10 minutes for well-done beef. Baste the beef with the pan juices every 15 minutes to ensure all-round flavour. Halfway through the cooking time, turn the meat and toss in the shallots, garlic and thyme.

While the meat is cooking, prepare the mash by putting parsnips and potatoes in a large pan. Cover with water and bring to the boil, then simmer until both are tender. This should take about 25-30 minutes, then drain and keep warm. Meanwhile, bring the milk to the boil and add the nutmeg. Add to the parsnips and potatoes and season to taste. Toss in the butter and beat with a hand-held mixer to a smooth purée. Keep warm until ready to serve.

To make the horseradish sauce, place the horseradish root in a large bowl with the mustard, vinegar, sugar, cream and chives. Whisk together vigorously and when it has reached a soft peak consistency, the sauce is ready. Transfer to a serving bowl, then cover with clingfilm and keep chilled until needed.

Once the beef is cooked, take it out of the oven and transfer from the roasting tin onto a carving platter. Cover the beef with foil and leave to rest for 20 minutes. Leave the shallots, garlic and thyme in the tin and place directly on the hob. Add the wine and reduce by half, stirring occasionally. Then add the stock and cook for another 2-3 minutes, then season to taste. Sieve into a clean pan and the gravy is ready. If you find the taste too sharp, add a pinch of sugar. Carve the beef into slices and arrange on warmed serving plates with the parsnip and potato mash and some steamed long stemmed broccoli. Put the gravy into a warmed gravy boat and place on the table with the horseradish sauce so that they can be handed around separately.

Best-Ever Homemade Beef Burger

Yes. I do call this the "best ever" home beef burger. I am nothing if not modest! And who doesn't enjoy a good, well-made beef burger. We all grab the fast food now and again, but really it is worth the effort to have the real thing. And don't be put off by the chilli mayonnaise. It gives it a bit of a kick without being too hot. By the way, this is the very burger our own staff eat nearly every week. That could be as many as twenty of us, before settling in to a night of cooking and meeting our guests. So it is definitely tried and tested.

Ingredients (Serves 6)

- 2 tbsp rapeseed oil
- 1 small onion, diced
- 2 garlic cloves, crushed
- 800g (1¾lb) lean minced beef
- 1 tbsp chopped fresh sage
- 1 egg, beaten
- 6 burger buns, split in half
- 50g (2oz) rocket
- 3 vine-ripened tomatoes, sliced

For the Chilli Mayonnaise:
- 100g (4oz) mayonnaise
- 1 tsp sweet chilli sauce (Thai Gold)
- Maldon sea salt and freshly ground black pepper

Method

First make the chilli mayonnaise. Place the mayonnaise and chilli sauce together in a bowl and mix until well combined. Season to taste. Cover with clingfilm and keep in the fridge until ready to serve.

Heat half the oil in a frying pan and add the onion and garlic. Sauté for 2-3 minutes until softened, then remove from the heat and leave to cool a little.

Place the minced beef in a bowl with the sage and egg. Add the onion mixture and mix well to combine, then season to taste. Divide the mixture into four portions and shape into burgers that are about 2.5cm (1in) thick. Chill for 20 minutes to allow the burgers to firm up.

Wipe out the frying pan and reheat with the rest of the oil. Add the burgers and cook for 6-7 minutes on each side until medium or longer if you prefer your meat more well done.

While the meat is cooking, preheat the grill and use to toast the burger buns. To serve, place a small amount of rocket, followed by the sliced tomatoes on the toasted bun base, then top with a beef burger. Drizzle the chilli mayonnaise over the whole burger and top with the remaining bun half to serve.

Chicken and Pork

Chicken and Vegetable Parcels with Oyster Sauce

This is a very easy cooking technique to master. In culinary terms it is what we call 'en papillote', which refers to a moist heat method where the food is enclosed in a packet of parchment paper or foil and then cooked, in the oven. When the parcel is fully cooked it will puff up so you know that the chicken and vegetables are completely tender inside.

Ingredients (Serves 4)

- 4 medium skinless chicken fillets, thinly sliced
- 2 garlic cloves, finely chopped
- 1 tsp finely grated root ginger
- 1 small red chilli, seeded and thinly sliced
- 2 tbsp dark soy sauce
- 2 tbsp oyster sauce
- small bunch fresh coriander, leaves picked
- 2 carrots, thinly sliced on the diagonal
- 1 red and 1 yellow pepper, seeded and cut into diamond shapes
- 175g (6oz) mangetout, topped and tailed
- 4 spring onions, thinly sliced on the diagonal
- 200g can water chestnuts, drained and thinly sliced
- cooked noodles or rice, to serve

Method

Toss the chicken, garlic, ginger, chilli, soy sauce, oyster sauce and a handful of coriander together in a medium bowl. Cover with clingfilm and leave to marinate for about 30 minutes in the fridge.

Preheat the oven to 180°C (350°F), Gas Mark 4. Cut out eight squares of parchment paper. Toss the carrots, peppers, mangetout, spring onions, water chestnuts and another handful of coriander together in a large bowl and divide between the squares of paper, placing them in the centre.

Divide the chicken and marinade mixture on top of the vegetables. Fold the paper over the chicken from all four sides to totally enclose the filling and form parcels, then place them seam-side down on a large baking sheet. Bake for 20 minutes until the vegetables and chicken are cooked through and the parcels are puffed up.

Arrange two parcels on each serving plate, turning them seam side up for each person to open. Serve with the noodles or rice in a warmed serving bowl so that everyone can help themselves.

Roast Chicken with Lemon, Garlic and Thyme

There is something very comforting about a whole roast chicken brought to the table – to me it reminds me of family Sunday lunches. The flavours here are fantastic and really penetrate the flesh of the chicken. Try to buy a free-range or organic chicken, as the flavour is always so much better.

Ingredients (Serves 4)

- 1.5kg (3lb) whole chicken
- 1 lemon
- 1 fresh thyme sprig
- 75g (3oz) butter, softened
- 2 garlic cloves, crushed
- 2 red onions, peeled and halved
- 4 small carrots, peeled
- 1 leek, chopped in half
- 2 celery sticks, chopped in half
- 1 garlic bulb, broken into cloves (but not peeled)
- 3 tbsp rapeseed oil
- 1 tbsp plain flour
- 120ml (4fl oz) white wine
- 600ml (1 pint) vegetable or chicken stock (see Essentials page 213 and 215)
- Maldon sea salt and freshly ground black pepper
- roast potatoes and buttered peas, to serve

Method

Take your chicken out of the fridge 30 minutes before it goes into the oven. Preheat the oven to 230°C (450°F), Gas mark 8. Finely grate the rind from the lemon into a bowl, reserving the lemon. Strip the thyme leaves from the stalks and add to the lemon rind. Mix in the butter with the garlic and then season to taste.

Loosen the skin from the chicken breasts starting at the cavity end and working your hand underneath to release.

Spread the butter evenly under the skin and lay the skin back down on top. Slash the chicken legs several times with a sharp knife (this is to help ensure crispy skin once cooked).

Place the red onions in a roasting tin with the carrots, leek, celery and garlic. Add one tablespoon of the oil and toss to coat. Sit the chicken on top of the pile of vegetables and drizzle all over with the remaining oil, then season well, rubbing it all over and right into the slashes.

Cut the reserved lemon in half and put it inside the chicken's cavity with the reserved thyme stalks. Place the chicken in the oven and immediately reduce the heat to 200°C (400°F), Gas mark 6. Roast the chicken for 1 hour and 20 minutes, basting the chicken halfway through cooking.

When the chicken is cooked, remove it from the oven, transfer it to a board and put the carrots and red onions on a warmed plate. Cover each with tin foil and leave to rest for 15 minutes while you make the gravy.

Using a large spoon, carefully remove most of the fat from the tin and then place the tin directly on the heat. Stir in the flour and then holding the tin steady, mash up the remaining vegetables as much as possible with a potato masher to release their juices.

Pour the wine into the tin and allow to reduce down, stirring continuously to blend in the flour. Pour in the stock and bring to the boil, then reduce the heat and simmer for about 10 minutes until slightly reduced and thickened, stirring occasionally. Take a large jug and set a sieve into it, then pour in the gravy and use a ladle to push all of the liquid and some of the vegetables through with the back of the spoon. Stir in the juices from the resting chicken and season to taste. Transfer to a warmed gravy boat.

Carve the chicken into slices and arrange on warmed serving plates with the reserved carrots and red onion halves, the roast potatoes and buttered peas. Pour over the gravy to serve.

Curried Chicken in Coconut Milk

I first tasted curried chicken in coconut milk in Thailand, which is one of my favourite places. This is not an overly spicy dish, so is good for introducing children to Asian foods and widening their palate. Thai Gold is a Wexford company that I came across during my work. They have the best of ingredients and are worth looking out for when you make this dish.

Ingredients (Serves 4-6)

- 1 tbsp sunflower oil
- 4 skinless chicken fillets, sliced
- 1 large onion, finely chopped
- 2 garlic cloves, finely chopped
- 1 tsp freshly grated root ginger
- 2 tsp Thai red curry paste (Thai Gold)
- 300ml (½ pint) chicken stock (see Essentials page 215)
- 400g can coconut milk (Thai Gold)
- 2 tsp caster sugar
- good pinch salt
- juice of 1 lime
- chopped fresh coriander leaves, to garnish
- Thai fragrant or basmati rice, to serve

Method

Heat a wok or large heavy-based frying pan until very hot. Add the oil and heat until it is almost smoking, swirling around the sides.

Tip the chicken breast into the heated wok and cook for a few minutes until lightly browned. Add the onion, garlic and ginger to the wok and cook for another 3-4 minutes until softened.

Stir the curry paste into the chicken mixture and cook for 2 minutes, stirring continuously. Pour in the chicken stock and coconut milk and bring to a gentle simmer. Stir in the sugar and salt, then add enough lime juice to taste and simmer gently for 10-15 minutes until the sauce has slightly reduced and the chicken is completely tender.

To serve, divide among warmed wide-rimmed bowls and serve on warmed plates with the Thai fragrant or basmati rice.

Chicken Casserole with Sweet Potatoes

When you are in the mood for a real winter warmer, this chicken casserole is full of flavour. You can't go far wrong with this recipe, everyone seems to love it. If you don't fancy using sweet potatoes or find them difficult to get hold of, use ordinary potatoes instead. Just cut them into larger chunks to prevent them from breaking up; better still use a waxy variety.

Ingredients (Serves 6-8)

- 12 rindless streaky bacon rashers
- 12 skinless and boneless chicken thighs
- 3 tbsp rapeseed oil
- 2 onions, cut into wedges
- 2 sweet potatoes, peeled and cut into cubes (preferably orange-fleshed)
- 2 garlic cloves, crushed
- 2 tbsp redcurrant jelly
- 120ml (4fl oz) red wine
- 450ml (¾ pint) chicken stock (see Essentials page 215)
- 1 tbsp chopped fresh flat-leaf parsley
- 1 tbsp toasted flaked almonds
- Maldon sea salt and freshly ground black pepper
- mashed potatoes, to serve

Method

Preheat the oven to 200°C (400°F), Gas mark 6. Stretch each rasher with the back of a table knife and then use to wrap around a chicken thigh. Heat the oil in a large casserole with a lid and cook the wrapped chicken thighs in batches until lightly browned all over. Arrange on a plate and set aside.

Reduce the heat of the pan, add the onions and sweet potatoes, then sauté for 5 minutes until golden. Add the garlic and cook for 1 minute, stirring to prevent the mixture sticking. Add the redcurrant jelly and then pour in red wine and stock. Bring to the boil, then reduce the heat and return the chicken to the casserole. Cover with the lid and cook in the oven for 1 hour or until the chicken is completely tender and the sauce has thickened slightly. Season to taste.

To serve, sprinkle the casserole with the parsley and flaked almonds, then place directly on the table with a large bowl of mash to mop up all those delicious juices.

Chicken Satay with Pickled Cucumber Salad

My brother, Kenneth, loves Asian food and he is without a doubt far better than me at cooking it! He is proud of this chicken satay dish and often makes it for the family. This dipping sauce also works well with pork, prawns, beef strips or turkey.

Ingredients (Serves 4)

- 4 tbsp dark soy sauce
- 2 tsp clear honey
- 2 tsp medium curry powder
- 450g (1lb) skinless chicken fillets, cut into long strips

For the Salad:
- 4 tbsp rice wine vinegar
- 2 tbsp caster sugar
- ½ small cucumber, peeled, halved, seeded and thinly sliced

For the Dipping Sauce:
- 2 tbsp crunchy peanut butter
- 2 tsp dark soy sauce
- 1 tsp light muscovado sugar
- juice of ½ lime
- 160ml can coconut milk (Thai Gold)
- ½ red chilli, seeded and finely diced
- 2 tbsp chopped fresh coriander
- Maldon sea salt and freshly ground black pepper

Method

Preheat a griddle pan until smoking hot. Whisk together the soy sauce, honey and curry powder. Season with pepper and stir in the chicken pieces. Leave to marinate for 2 minutes. Thread the chicken pieces on to 8x 15cm (6in) bamboo skewers and arrange on the griddle pan. Cook the chicken skewers for 4-6 minutes until completely tender and cooked through, turning once or twice.

Meanwhile, prepare the pickled cucumber salad. Place the vinegar in a bowl and stir in the sugar and a good pinch of salt until dissolved. Tip in the cucumber, stirring to combine and set aside to allow the flavours to develop.

To make the dipping sauce. Place the peanut butter in a small pan and stir in the soy sauce, light muscovado sugar and lime juice. Gradually whisk in the coconut milk and heat gently until you have achieved a smooth sauce. Stir in the chilli and coriander, then leave to cool, stirring occasionally to prevent a skin forming.

Arrange two chicken satay skewers on each warmed serving plate. Divide the dipping sauce among individual dipping bowls and place to the side of the skewers. Add the pickled cucumber salad, leaving behind any excess liquid and serve at once.

Chicken Tikka Wraps

Try to marinate the chicken earlier in the day or better still the night before as the flavour will really have a chance to penetrate and tenderise the flesh. If you don't want to buy this selection of spices try using a heaped teaspoon of curry powder or paste.

Ingredients (Serves 4)

- 150g (5oz) natural yoghurt
- 1 garlic clove, crushed
- 1 tsp ground cumin
- ½ tsp cayenne pepper
- ½ tsp ground turmeric
- 4 small skinless chicken breast fillets
- 4 soft flour tortilla wraps
- 4 large iceberg lettuce leaves, shredded
- Maldon sea salt and freshly ground black pepper
- lime wedges, to garnish

Method

Place the yoghurt in a bowl and add the garlic, cumin, cayenne pepper and turmeric. Season to taste and mix until well combined. Cut the chicken breast fillets into thin strips and stir into the yoghurt mixture. Cover with clingfilm and set aside to marinate in the fridge for at least 20 minutes or up to 24 hours, if time allows.

Preheat the grill. Arrange the yoghurt-coated chicken strips on a foil-lined grill rack and cook for about 6 minutes, turning occasionally until cooked through and lightly golden.

Meanwhile, warm the tortilla wraps in the microwave or on a dry, heated frying pan for about 15 seconds on each side. Divide the chicken tikka among the warmed tortilla wraps and scatter with shredded lettuce. To serve, roll up tightly, and then wrap in greaseproof paper to pack for lunch boxes or cut on the diagonal and arrange on serving plates and garnish with the lime wedges.

Balsamic and Honey-Glazed Chicken Bake

This is a dish that is worth thinking about a day ahead. The marinade will improve the flavour with time, as it penetrates and flavours the meat. You could also make this meal with chicken or turkey legs, which are very lean and good value, just amend the cooking times accordingly.

Ingredients (Serves 4)

- 4 chicken fillets (skin on)
- 2 carrots, thickly sliced
- 675g (1½lb) baby potatoes, halved
- 2 tbsp rapeseed oil
- 1 tbsp chopped fresh flat-leaf parsley

For the Marinade:

- 5 tbsp clear honey
- 1 tbsp tomato ketchup
- 2 tbsp balsamic vinegar
- 2 tbsp soy sauce
- Maldon sea salt and freshly ground black pepper
- lightly dressed green salad, to serve

Method

To make the marinade, mix the honey, tomato ketchup, balsamic vinegar and soy sauce in a small non-metallic dish until smooth. Add the chicken, turning to coat and then cover with clingfilm and leave to marinade for at least 3 hours or overnight in the fridge is best.

Once the meat is marinated, preheat the oven to 220°C (425°F), Gas mark 7. Bring two pans of salted water to the boil and cook the carrots for 6-8 minutes in one and the baby potatoes for 10-15 minutes in the other until par-cooked. Drain the vegetables well and season to taste. Toss in half of the oil and arrange in an ovenproof dish.

Meanwhile, heat the remaining oil in a frying pan on a high heat. Remove the chicken from the marinade (reserving it to use again later) and sear skin-side down for 1 minute until golden brown, then flip over and do the other side for another minute. Place the chicken on top of the vegetables, skin-side up, and roast in the oven for about 15 minutes until the chicken and vegetables are cooked through and tender.

In the meantime, pour the remaining marinade into a small pan and simmer gently for a few minutes or until slightly reduced and thickened. About 5 minutes before the end of cooking time, brush the chicken all over with the reduced down marinade and return to the oven to glaze. Scatter over the parsley and serve straight to the table with some green salad to hand around separately.

Turkey and Leek Pot Pie

This rustic turkey and leek pie uses a favourite cut of mine: turkey steaks. They are always good value, and very low in fat. I like to eat this with a big bowl of salad. And the ready made rolled puff pastry in your supermarket makes this a very convenient dish; perfect for a cold winters evening.

Ingredients (Serves 4-6)

- 2 tbsp rapeseed oil
- 450g (1lb) turkey steaks, cut into 2.5cm (1in) strips on the diagonal
- 2 potatoes, cut into cubes
- 4 leeks, trimmed and thickly sliced
- 1 tsp chopped fresh thyme
- 1 tbsp plain flour
- 100g (4oz) frozen petit pois
- 300ml (½ pint) crème fraîche
- 300ml (½ pint) chicken stock (see Essentials page 215)
- 2 tbsp chopped fresh flat-leaf parsley
- 375g packet ready-rolled puff pastry, thawed if frozen
- 1 egg, beaten
- Maldon sea salt and freshly ground black pepper
- steamed broccoli florets, to serve

Method

Preheat the oven to 190°C (375°F), Gas mark 5. Put the oil in a roasting tin or large pie dish. Add the turkey strips, potatoes, leeks, thyme and flour. Toss well together and season to taste. Roast for 25 minutes until tender, turning the turkey and vegetables occasionally to ensure they cook evenly.

Remove the roasting tin from the oven and fold in the frozen petit pois. Then stir in the crème fraîche, chicken stock and parsley. Leave to cool slightly. Lay the pastry over the pie dish, tuck in the edges down around the sides. Brush the rim with water to help it stick and then brush the top of pie with beaten egg to glaze.

Bake the turkey and leek pie in the oven for 25-30 minutes until the pastry has risen and is golden and the chicken and vegetables are tender. Reduce the temperature of the oven if the pie is browning too quickly.

To serve, bring the pie directly to the table and serve on warmed serving plates, handing around a bowl of the steamed broccoli florets so that everyone can help themselves.

Stuffed Roast Goose with Braised Red Cabbage and Potato Gratin

This stuffed roast goose is what we always have as a family for Christmas dinner, served with all of the trimmings. Free-range geese are usually in plentiful supply during the festive period. Goose is a little more expensive but it is only one day of the year. If you decide to make the potato gratin while the goose is cooking you will need two ovens. Alternatively make the potato gratin the day before, then once cooled, cover and chill until needed. Cut into portions and reheat in the bottom shelf of the oven for about 30 minutes before serving.

Ingredients (Serves 8-10)

- 4.25kg (12lb) oven-ready goose, at room temperature
- 1 tsp salt
- 2 tbsp redcurrant jelly
- 1 tbsp balsamic vinegar
- 1 tbsp ruby red port or red wine
- finely grated rind of 1 orange

For the Stuffing:
- 2 tbsp rapeseed oil
- 2 eating apples, peeled, cored and cut into thin slices
- 1 tbsp chopped fresh thyme, plus extra sprigs to garnish
- 350g (12oz) sausage meat (good quality)
- 75g (3oz) fresh white breadcrumbs
- 100g (4oz) dried cranberries
- 100g (4oz) walnut halves, chopped

For the Red Cabbage:
- 1 tbsp sunflower oil
- 50g (2oz) smoked bacon, rind removed and diced

- 1 head of red cabbage, tough cores removed and finely sliced
- 1 tsp ground cinnamon
- 1 tsp mixed spice
- 1 tsp ground cloves
- 2 tbsp balsamic vinegar
- 4 tbsp light brown sugar
- 300ml (½ pint) red wine
- 300ml (½ pint) apple juice
- 2 cooking apples, peeled, cored and chopped

For the Potato Gratin:
- 400ml (14fl oz) milk
- 300ml (½ pint) double cream
- 4 garlic cloves, crushed
- good pinch freshly grated nutmeg
- 8 rindless smoked streaky bacon rashers
- 900g (2lb) potatoes, cut into wafer-thin slices
- butter, for greasing
- 100g (4oz) Cheddar cheese, grated
- Maldon sea salt and freshly ground black pepper
- Madeira sauce, to serve (see Essentials page 196)

Method

To make the stuffing, heat the oil in a large frying pan. Add the apples and sauté them for 3-4 minutes until softened and golden. Transfer to a bowl and leave to cool. Once cool, add the thyme, sausage meat, breadcrumbs, cranberries and walnuts, stirring gently until evenly mixed. Season to taste.

Preheat oven to 200°C (400°F), Gas mark 6. Place the goose on a rack set over a roasting tin. Pour over a full kettle of boiling water, then drain off the water from the roasting tin. To stuff the goose, start at the neck end, where you'll find a flap of loose skin. Gently loosen this away from the breast, and you'll be able to make a triangular pocket. Pack two-thirds of the stuffing inside as far as you can go, and make a neat round shape on the outside, then tuck the neck flap under the goose and secure it with a small skewer. Rub all over with salt.

Press the remaining stuffing into the base of a 225g (8oz) loaf tin and set aside. Weigh the goose and calculate the cooking time, allowing 15 minutes per 450g (1lb) plus 15 minutes. This goose should take about 3½ hours. Place in the oven to roast, draining off excess fat every 30 minutes or so and, after 1 hour, reduce the oven temperature to 180°C (350°F), Gas mark 4. Continue to cook, still draining the fat off every half an hour.

Meanwhile, make the red cabbage. Heat the oil in a heavy-based pan over a high heat. Add the bacon and sauté for 30 seconds, then add the cabbage and spices, stirring to combine. Reduce the heat and cook for 8-10 minutes, until the cabbage is well cooked down, adding a tablespoon or two of water if the cabbage starts to catch on the bottom. Add the vinegar, sugar, wine and apple juice. Give a good stir, then cover with a lid and simmer for 1 hour over a low heat, stirring occasionally. Stir in the apples and cook gently for another 30 minutes, again stirring occasionally. Season to taste and keep warm over a low heat.

To prepare the potato gratin, preheat a separate oven to 160°C (325°F), Gas mark 3. Pour the milk and cream into a pan and add the garlic and nutmeg. Season to taste and just heat through, but do not allow the mixture to boil, then quickly remove from the heat.

Meanwhile, preheat the grill. Arrange the bacon rashers on a grill rack to cook for about five minutes, until crisp and lightly golden, turning once. Drain on kitchen paper and, when cool enough to handle, snip into pieces with scissors. Arrange a third of the potatoes in a greased ovenproof dish of about 23cm (9in) x 18cm (7in) and 5cm (2in) deep. Season to taste and scatter over half of the bacon, then add another third of the potatoes in an even layer. Season to taste and scatter over the remaining bacon.

Arrange the rest of the potatoes on top in an attractive overlapping layer, and carefully pour over the milk mixture. Cover the potato gratin with a piece of foil and sit on a baking sheet. Bake for 1 hour and 15 minutes, until cooked through and lightly golden, then remove the foil. Sprinkle over the Cheddar and return to the oven for another 5 minutes or until the Cheddar is bubbling and golden brown.

Remove the goose from the oven 30 minutes before the end of the cooking time. Warm the redcurrant jelly, balsamic vinegar, port or wine and orange rind in a small pan. Bring to a simmer, stirring until the jelly dissolves, then cook for 4-5 minutes, until syrupy. Brush all over the goose. Return the goose to the oven with the reserved tin of extra stuffing and cook for the final 30 minutes until completely tender. Transfer the goose to a serving platter and cover with foil, then leave to rest for 10 minutes. Spoon

the stuffing into a warmed bowl and keep warm.

To serve, garnish the roast goose with the thyme and bring to the table. Turn the tin of extra stuffing onto a warmed plate. Carve the goose into slices and arrange on warmed plates, then drizzle with the Madeira sauce. Add some of the stuffing to each plate with the braised red cabbage and potato gratin.

Roast Rack of Pork with Apples

Ask your butcher for this rack of pork as he will remove the chine bone and trim the joint so that it is ready for the oven. Make sure the crackling is on and add some sea salt to make it crispy. I like the nice aniseed taste of fennel seeds which I have put in the marinade but of course you could leave them out. Leftovers are very good cold in a sandwich with the stuffed apple mashed up.

Ingredients (Serves 10)

- 2.25-2.75kg (5-6lb) rack of pork, chined and rind scored
- 8-10 red eating apples
- 16-20 prunes, stones removed and quartered
- 200ml (7fl oz) white wine
- 10 small parsnips
- 10 carrots
- 10 potatoes, halved
- 10 red onions
- 3 tbsp rapeseed oil
- 2-3 tbsp runny honey

For the Marinade

- 2 tbsp rapeseed oil
- 2-3 garlic cloves, finely chopped
- 1 tsp fennel seeds, toasted
- juice and finely grated rind of 1 lemon
- Maldon sea salt and freshly ground black pepper

Method

A day ahead, if possible, marinade the pork. Mix the oil, garlic, fennel seeds, lemon juice and rind together in a small bowl. Place the pork into a shallow non-metallic dish that will fit into the fridge comfortably. Spread over the marinade and then cover with clingfilm. Leave in the fridge overnight to allow the flavours to penetrate into the flesh or up to two days is fine.

Preheat the oven to 200°C (400°F), Gas mark 6. Place the pork in a large roasting tin, then season well and roast for two hours. Reduce the oven temperature if necessary when the crackling is crisp and well browned. Core the apples and then stuff the cavities with the prunes. Add the stuffed apples to the pork with the wine and return to the oven. Continue cooking for another 35-40 minutes until the pork and apples are fully cooked.

Toss the parsnips, carrots, potatoes and onions in the oil in a separate roasting tin and season to taste, then place on the top shelf above the pork. Roast for 45-50 minutes until the vegetables are tender and just beginning to caramelise.

Twenty minutes before the end of cooking time, drizzle the pork, apples and vegetables with the runny honey. To serve, lift the pork and apples out of the roasting tray and leave to rest for 15 minutes. Boil up the juices with a knob of butter, then season to taste. Carve the pork and arrange on serving plates with the stuffed apples and roasted vegetables to serve.

Pork Pitta Pockets

Of course you can use a frying pan for this recipe but it is so much better to use a good non-stick wok. If you buy a good quality one, it should last you for years. You will get one for €30-40 and, incidentally, it is a great gift for a student about to embark on college life.

Ingredients (Serves 4)

- 450g (1lb) pork fillet, trimmed and cut into thin strips
- 2 tbsp rapeseed oil
- 2 peppers, seeded and thinly sliced
- 4 white pitta breads (oval shaped)
- 6 tbsp mayonnaise or Greek-style yoghurt
- 2 tsp chopped fresh mint
- 40g (1½oz) mixed salad leaves
- squeeze of lemon juice

For the Spicy Marinade
- 1 tbsp mild curry paste
- 1 tbsp rapeseed oil
- Maldon sea salt and freshly ground black pepper

Method

Mix the curry paste with the oil in a bowl large enough to take the pork and season to taste. Add the pork and mix well to combine, then leave at room temperature for 5 minutes if time allows.

Heat a non-stick wok or heavy-based frying pan until smoking hot. Add the pork and sauté for 3-4 minutes until cooked through and lightly golden. Tip onto a plate. Add one tablespoon of the oil to the frying pan and sauté the peppers for about 5 minutes until softened and just beginning to catch around the edges, adding a tablespoon or two of water to help them cook.

Meanwhile, toast the pitta breads and split open. Place the mayonnaise or yoghurt in a bowl and season to taste, then stir in the mint. Toss the salad leaves in the rest of the oil and the lemon juice. Use to fill the pittas. Tip the pork back into the wok and allow to just warm through, then use to stuff the pitta breads. Drizzle over the mint mayonnaise and serve at once on warmed serving plates.

Toulouse Sausages with Red Onion Gravy and Creamy Apple and Potato Mash

The increase in people who are eating sausages regularly and also the number of restaurants serving them now is amazing! There are so many interesting and tasty sausages easily available now. I like them to have a natural casing and a high meat content. Toulouse sausages are French in origin and normally are more coarsely minced and flavoured with garlic, wine and plenty of seasonings.

Ingredients (Serves 4)

- 900g (2lb) potatoes, cut into chunks
- 1 tbsp sunflower oil
- 8 large Toulouse pork sausages
- 75g (3oz) butter
- 1 eating apple, peeled, cored and diced
- 100ml (3½fl oz) milk

For the Red Onion Gravy:

- 25g (1oz) butter
- 450g (1lb) red onions, halved and thinly sliced
- ½ tsp sugar
- 150ml (¼ pint) red wine
- 1 tbsp plain flour
- 300ml (½ pint) beef stock (see Essentials page 214)
- Maldon sea salt and freshly ground black pepper
- fresh thyme leaves, to garnish
- Dijon mustard, to serve

Method

To make the gravy, melt the butter in a large frying pan and add the onions and sugar, then cook over a medium heat for 20-30 minutes until caramelised, stirring occasionally. Pour in the wine and allow to reduce down, then simmer for about 4-5 minutes until all the liquid has gone. Add in the flour and cook for 1 minute, stirring. Gradually stir in the stock, then season to taste and simmer gently for 4-5 minutes until you have achieved a thick, rich gravy. Keep warm.

Meanwhile, make the creamy apple and potato mash. Place the potatoes in a pan of boiling salted water and simmer for 15-20 minutes or until tender. After about 10 minutes, heat the oil in a frying pan. Cook the sausages for about 10 minutes until golden brown, turning regularly. Place 25g (1oz) of the butter in a small pan with the apple and cook gently for 4-5 minutes until the apple is completely soft, stirring occasionally, and then mash down with a fork.

Drain the potatoes and mash until smooth. Heat the milk and remaining butter in a small pan. Beat the apple mixture into the mashed potatoes with the hot milk mixture. Season to taste. Divide the creamy apple and potato mash among warmed plates and arrange the sausages alongside. Spoon over the onion gravy. Garnish with the thyme leaves and add a good dollop of Dijon mustard to each plate to serve.

Bacon Carbonara

Of course, this bacon carbonara can be made with pastas other than spaghetti. You might try penne, linguini or tagliatelle, and they will all have the cooking instructions on the packet. It is a good, tasty meal to impress someone. You might even add a glass of red wine and a candle!

Ingredients (Serves 4)

- 350g (12oz) spaghetti
- 25g (1oz) butter
- 1 onion, finely chopped
- 1 garlic clove, crushed
- 225g (8oz) pancetta or rindless bacon rashers, cubed
- 100ml (3½fl oz) white wine
- 3 eggs
- 150ml (¼ pint) double cream
- 50g (2oz) freshly grated Parmesan cheese, plus extra to serve
- 1 tbsp chopped fresh flat-leaf parsley
- Maldon sea salt and freshly ground black pepper

Method

Bring a large pan of salted water to a rolling boil and then swirl in the spaghetti. Cook the pasta for 8-10 minutes or until just tender but still with a little bite - 'al dente'.

Meanwhile, heat the butter in a large pan. Add the onion and garlic and cook over a low heat for 5 minutes until softened but not coloured, stirring frequently. Add the pancetta or bacon to the pan and cook for another 6-8 minutes until crisp, stirring continuously.

Pour the wine into the bacon mixture and reduce the liquid to about one tablespoon. Crack the eggs into a bowl and add the cream and Parmesan cheese. Season with plenty of freshly ground black pepper and beat until well combined.

Drain the pasta and return it to the pan and then tip in the pancetta mixture. Pour over the beaten egg mixture and add the parsley. Cook gently for a minute until the sauce thickens slightly. Be careful not to overcook the sauce or the eggs will scramble! Divide among warmed serving plates and add a good grinding of black pepper to each one. Scatter over a little more Parmesan cheese to serve.

Smoked Bacon and Pea Risotto

Smoked bacon and pea risotto is very simple to make and a great mid-week meal. Arborio and Carnaroli rice are both Italian short-grain rice and their rounded grains are nice and chewy due to the higher starch content. Use leftovers to make risotto cakes - crunchy on the outside and rich and creamy in the middle. Simply, roll and flatten handfuls of cold risotto into patties. Coat in a mixture of breadcrumbs and freshly grated Parmesan before frying in butter until golden.

Ingredients (Serves 4-6)

- 1.2 litres (2 pints) chicken stock (see Essentials page 215)
- 25g (1oz) butter
- 4 smoked bacon rashers, rinds removed and diced
- 1 small onion, diced
- 1 garlic clove, crushed
- 300g (11oz) Arborio or Carnaroli rice (risotto)
- 100g (4oz) fresh or frozen peas
- 75g (3oz) freshly grated Parmesan cheese, plus extra shavings to garnish
- 1 tbsp chopped fresh flat-leaf parsley and chives
- Maldon sea salt and freshly ground black pepper

Method

Pour the stock into a large pan and bring to a gentle simmer. Melt the butter in a large heavy-based frying pan. Add the bacon and sauté for 2 minutes, then add the onion and garlic and sauté for another 2 minutes.

Add the rice to the bacon mixture and continue to cook for another minute, stirring to ensure that all the grains are well coated. Begin to add the simmering stock a ladle at a time, stirring frequently. Allow each stock addition to be almost completely absorbed before adding the next.

After 15 minutes cooking, stir in the peas and continue to cook as before. Then after approximately 20 minutes when all of the stock has been absorbed and the rice is 'al dente' – firm but still with a little bite, add the Parmesan and herbs and then stir well to combine. Season to taste and divide among warmed serving plates and garnish with the Parmesan shavings. Serve immediately.

Fish

Baked Smoked Haddock Pasta

Pasta has become very popular in recent years. It is handy to buy and keep in the cupboard and so versatile to use. In the restaurant, we make our own pasta, but at home I tend to use De Cecco, which I think is very good quality. It is the one in the blue-and-white pack. Instead of spaghetti, you could also use linguini or penne. Go to your local fishmonger and you will get good natural smoked haddock.

Ingredients (Serves 4)

- 4 dry cured bacon rashers, rinds removed
- 350g (12oz) spaghetti
- 200ml (7fl oz) milk
- 350g (12oz) smoked haddock fillet, skinned
- 2 eggs
- 3 tbsp crème fraîche
- 2 tsp Dijon mustard
- 50g (2oz) vintage Cheddar cheese, finely grated
- Maldon sea salt and freshly ground black pepper
- dressed mixed salad leaves, to serve

Method

Preheat the oven to 190°C (375°F), Gas mark 5. Place the bacon on a small non-stick baking tin and cook for 10 minutes or until lightly crisp, then remove and roughly chop into pieces.

Cook the pasta in a large pan of boiling water for 10-12 minutes until tender but still with a little bite-'al dente'; or according to packet instructions.

Bring the milk to the boil in a pan, then lower the heat and add the smoked haddock. Poach for 3-4 minutes until just tender. Remove with a slotted spoon and when cool enough to handle, lightly flake the flesh into a bowl, discarding any bones. Strain the poaching milk into a bowl and allow to cool slightly. Add the eggs, crème fraîche, mustard and half the Cheddar, then season to taste. Fold in the flaked smoked haddock and bacon and mix gently together to combine.

Drain the spaghetti and return to the pan and then stir in the smoked haddock and cream mixture. Tip into an ovenproof baking dish and scatter over the remaining Cheddar. Bake for 20-25 minutes until just set and the top is bubbling and golden. Serve straight to the table with a separate bowl of lightly dressed mixed salad.

Fish and Chips

Not just a take-away, this dish can be made at home without too much effort. Fierce battles rage over how best to coat the fish, but I have to say this particular way of coating the fish in breadcrumbs gives a lovely crisp result.

Ingredients (Serves 4)

- 2 litres (3½ pints) sunflower oil
- 900g (2lb) floury potatoes, such as Desiree or King Edward
- 4 x 175g (6oz) cod fillets, boned and skinned
- 100g (4oz) plain flour
- 2 eggs, beaten
- 200g (7oz) fresh white breadcrumbs
- 1 tsp chopped fresh flat-leaf parsley
- 1 tsp sesame seeds
- Maldon sea salt and freshly ground black pepper
- lime wedges, to garnish

Method

Preheat the oven to 150°C (300°F), Gas mark 2. Pour all the sunflower oil into a deep-fat fryer or a deep-sided pan, making sure it is only half full, and heat to 160°C (325°F). Cut the potatoes into chunky chips, about 2cm (¾in) thick and then place in a bowl of cold water - this helps to remove the starch. Drain and then dry them as much as possible in a clean tea towel before placing them in a wire basket (you may need to do this in two batches depending on the size of your basket) and lowering them into the heated oil. Cook for 4 minutes until cooked through but not coloured. Drain well on kitchen paper and set aside.

Increase the temperature of the oil to 190°C (375°F) and prepare the fish. Place the flour on a flat plate and season to taste. Put the beaten eggs and some seasoning in a shallow dish and mix the breadcrumbs with the parsley and sesame seeds in another separate dish.

Coat the cod fillets in the flour, shaking off any excess and then dip into the beaten egg and finally coat in the breadcrumbs. Quickly place in the heated oil and cook for 5-6 minutes until crisp and golden brown - the exact time will depend on the thickness of the fillets (again you may have to do this in two batches). Drain on kitchen paper and keep warm in the oven - this should only be for a minute or two so the batter doesn't loose any of its crispness.

Tip the blanched chips back into the wire basket and then carefully lower into the heated oil. Cook for one to two minutes until crisp and golden brown. Drain well on kitchen paper and season with salt, then serve immediately with the fish on warmed serving plates. Garnish with the lime wedges and serve the bowl of salad separately so that everyone can help themselves.

Mackerel with Sherry Vinaigrette and New Potato Salad

Mackerel is a great value fish and here in Blacklion we are fortunate in being only half an hour from Bundoran so it available freshly caught and ready to go. Mackerel must be eaten fresh. It is an oil-rich fish that is naturally low in saturated fat, full of vitamins and minerals, and an excellent source of essential omega 3 fats. The body cannot make omega 3 fats so to ensure you get a regular supply, you should eat oil-rich fish – like mackerel, salmon or trout – once a week.

Ingredients (Serves 4)

- 4 mackerel fillets, skin on and pin bones removed
- 2 tbsp rapeseed oil

For the Vinaigrette:
- 2 tbsp sherry vinegar
- 4 tbsp extra-virgin rapeseed oil
- 1 tsp golden syrup
- 1 tsp wholegrain mustard
- pinch light brown sugar

For the Potato Salad:
- 900g (2lb) waxy new potatoes, scraped or scrubbed (preferably small)
- 2 tsp white wine vinegar
- 2 tbsp light rapeseed oil
- 4 tbsp mayonnaise
- 2 tbsp crème fraîche
- 1 bunch spring onions, trimmed and thinly sliced
- 2 tbsp chopped fresh dill
- 2 tbsp chopped fresh flat-leaf parsley
- Maldon sea salt and freshly ground black pepper
- wild rocket leaves, to serve

Method

First make the potato salad. If necessary, cut the potatoes into 2.5cm (1in) chunks. Place in a pan of salted water, bring to the boil and cook for 12-15 minutes or until tender. Meanwhile, whisk together the white wine vinegar in a large bowl with the oil and season to taste. Drain the potatoes well, toss into this dressing and leave to cool completely.

Meanwhile, make the sherry vinaigrette for the mackerel. Place the vinegar in a screw-topped jar with the oil, golden syrup, mustard and sugar. Season to taste and shake vigorously until emulsified. Set aside until needed.

To cook the mackerel, heat the oil in a non-stick frying pan. Season the mackerel fillets and to prevent them from curling up, make small incisions in the skin. Add to the heated oil and cook for 5-7 minutes, turning once until the skin is crisp and the mackerel is cooked through. To finish the potato salad, stir the mayonnaise and crème fraîche together in a small bowl and stir into the potatoes with the spring onions, dill, parsley and season to taste. This will keep very well in the fridge for up to 24 hours.

To serve, place the mackerel fillets on warmed serving plates. Drizzle the sherry vinaigrette around the plate, garnish with rocket leaves and serve with new potato salad.

Mussel Risotto with Leeks and Courgettes

This is a standard risotto recipe and one that you might like to vary according to taste. You could try other shellfish such as prawns. Alternatively you could have it as a vegetarian dish. Risotto is one of Italy's great simple dishes, rice cooked in broth to a creamy consistency. It is the perfect comfort food and always very popular in the restaurant. This risotto is a great dinner party or lunch dish. The trick of a good risotto is to add the stock little by little, allowing the liquid to almost disappear before adding the next ladleful.

Ingredients (Serves 4)

- 900g (2lb) fresh mussels, cleaned
- 1 onion, thinly sliced
- 1 leek, trimmed and diced
- 150ml (¼ pint) white wine
- 1.2 litres (2 pints) vegetable stock (see Essentials page 213)
- 1 tbsp rapeseed oil
- 225g (8oz) Arborio or Carnolini rice (risotto)
- 1 small courgette, diced
- 2 garlic cloves, crushed
- 4 tbsp chopped fresh mixed herbs, plus extra to garnish (such as chives and flat-leaf parsley)
- 1 tbsp freshly grated Parmesan, plus extra Parmesan shavings to garnish
- Maldon sea salt and freshly ground black pepper

Method

Heat a large pan and place the mussels in it. Add the onion with half of the leek and then pour in the wine and vegetable stock. Bring to the boil and then reduce the heat and simmer for a minute or two until all of the mussels have opened. Remove from the heat and pass the stock through a large sieve or colander. Remove the mussel meat from their shells and reserve; discarding any that have not opened.

Strain the stock into a clean pan, leaving behind any grit and bring to a gentle simmer. Heat the oil in a large sauté pan. Stir in the rice and stir for one minute until the grains are glossy. Add the rest of the leek with the courgette and garlic, stirring to combine. Pour a ladleful of the stock into the rice mixture and allow to bubble away, stirring. Continue to add the simmering stock a ladleful at a time, stirring frequently. Allow each stock addition to be almost completely absorbed before adding the next ladleful, until the rice is 'al dente' - tender on the outside, but still with a slight bite in the centre of the grain. This should take about 20 minutes.

Remove the risotto from the heat and stir in the herbs and Parmesan, then cover and leave to rest for 5 minutes. Stir in the cooked mussel meat and allow to heat through. Season to taste and divide among warmed serving plates. Garnish with herbs to serve.

Aromatic Fish Cakes with Lemon Mayonnaise

Fish cakes are a great, easy way to introduce kids to fish. Smoked haddock is a favourite in our household. Try and get natural, undyed smoked haddock. Frank Hederman in West Cork, in my opinion, has got to have one of the best smokehouses in the country. Feel free to add vegetables to the fishcakes; peas, carrots or sweetcorn would be good.

Ingredients (Serves 8)

- 1kg (2¼lb) floury potatoes, diced
- 400g (14oz) natural smoked haddock
- 300ml (½ pint) milk
- 1 tsp mild curry paste
- 1 bunch spring onions, trimmed and thinly sliced
- 1 tbsp chopped fresh coriander
- 1 tbsp chopped fresh flat-leaf parsley
- 100g (4oz) plain flour
- 4 eggs, beaten
- 250g (9oz) natural breadcrumbs
- 2 tbsp sesame seeds
- 4 tbsp sunflower oil

For the Mayonnaise:
- 100g (4oz) mayonnaise
- squeeze of lemon juice
- 2 tbsp snipped fresh chives
- Maldon sea salt and freshly ground black pepper
- lightly dressed mixed salad leaves, to serve
- lime wedges, to garnish

Method

Boil the potatoes in a large pan of boiling salted water for 15-20 minutes or until tender. Meanwhile, place the smoked haddock in a large pan. Pour over the milk and then cover and bring to the boil. Remove from the heat and leave the fish to finish cooking in the hot milk.

Drain the potatoes and return to the pan, then mash well until smooth. Beat in the curry paste, spring onions and herbs. Transfer the cooked smoked haddock to a plate with a fish slice. Break up the flesh into rough flakes, discarding any skin and bones. Gently fold into the mashed potato mixture. Season to taste. Using a small ice-cream scoop, shape the haddock and potato mixture into even-sized balls. Then, using slightly wet hands, shape into 16 x 1cm (½in) thick patties.

Arrange the haddock cakes on a baking sheet and leave to cool completely, then cover with clingfilm and chill for at least two hours – or overnight is best – to allow the fish cakes to firm up.

Place the flour on a plate and season generously. Put the beaten egg into a shallow dish, with the breadcrumbs and sesame seeds in a separate dish. Dust the chilled fish cakes in the seasoned flour and then carefully dip them in beaten egg. Finally, coat in the sesame breadcrumbs.

Heat the oil in a large heavy-based frying pan and shallow fry the fish cakes in batches for about 4-5 minutes on each side until crisp and golden. Drain well on kitchen paper and keep warm. Quickly mix the mayonnaise with the lemon juice and chives in a bowl. Season to taste.

To serve, arrange the fish cakes on warmed serving plates with the mixed salad leaves, and add a dollop of the lemon mayonnaise to each one. Garnish with the lime wedges.

Baked Salmon with Herbs and Citrus Fruit

Communion and Confirmation are great events for family and friends, and you want to be able to fully enjoy the day without worrying too much about the food. So I think buffet dishes are ideal, as much of the preparation can be done ahead to reduce the pressure on the day. This dish is just perfect for an occasion such as this or even around Christmas when you have a lot of people around that need feeding!

Ingredients (Serves 6-8)

- 175g (6oz) couscous
- finely grated rind and juice of 1 lemon and 1 lime
- 1 red onion, finely chopped
- 1 garlic clove, finely chopped
- 1 tbsp chopped rinsed capers
- 2 tbsp chopped fresh flat-leaf parsley
- 1 tbsp chopped fresh tarragon
- 1 egg, beaten
- 2 tbsp rapeseed oil
- 1 x 2kg (4½lb) whole salmon, skinned and filleted
- Maldon sea salt and freshly ground black pepper
- lemon wedges, to serve

Method

Preheat oven to 180°C (350°F), Gas mark 4. Place the couscous in a large bowl and pour over 250ml (9fl oz) of boiling water. Cover with clingfilm and leave to soak for about 5 minutes until all the water has been absorbed.

Fluff the couscous up with a fork, then stir in the lemon and lime rind and juice, red onion, garlic, capers, parsley and tarragon. Finally, stir in the egg and season well. Line a baking sheet with tin foil and drizzle over the oil.

Place one of the salmon fillets, skinned side down, on the oiled foil. Spread the couscous mixture evenly on top, pressing it into place. Lay the remaining salmon fillet on top of the stuffing, skinned side up. Bring the edges of the foil together over the salmon and scrunch the edges to seal, making sure the foil does not touch the top of the fish. Bake in the oven for 45 minutes, then leave to cool in the foil before removing and carefully transferring to a large serving platter. Garnish with lemon wedges and serve straight to the table.

Grilled Plaice with Lemon Butter and Caper Sauce

For a special occasion, substitute the plaice for Dover sole; otherwise small brill fillets or lemon sole would work well. This is one sauce that you really need to make your own stock for, as stock cubes are just too salty. Alternatively try using the cartons of chilled stocks available in most supermarkets. Too hot and the sauce will boil and split; too cold and the fat will set, again causing the sauce to split. To find the perfect temperature, it's best just to stick your finger in – it should feel warm, not hot.

Ingredients (Serves 4)

- 300ml (½ pint) chicken or vegetable stock (see Essentials page 213)
- 4 large plaice fillets, each about 250-275g (9-10oz)
- 100g (4oz) unsalted butter, diced and chilled
- ½ lemon, pips removed
- 1 tbsp snipped fresh chives
- 2 tbsp rinsed capers
- Maldon sea salt and freshly ground white pepper
- boiled baby potatoes and/or dressed crisp green salad, to serve

Method

Preheat the grill. To make the lemon and caper sauce, place the chicken or vegetable stock in a pan and reduce to two tablespoons. Arrange the plaice fillets on a non-stick baking sheet and dot with a little of the butter, then season to taste. Place directly under the grill for 10-12 minutes, without turning, until just cooked through and tender.

When the stock has reduced down sufficiently, turn the heat right down to its lowest setting and whisk in (or use a hand-blender to mix) the remaining butter, a few cubes at a time, until the butter has melted and the texture is light and frothy. Add a squeeze of lemon juice, then stir in the chives and capers. Season to taste.

Carefully transfer the plaice fillets onto warmed serving plates with a fish slice. Spoon the lemon and caper butter sauce on top to serve. Serve with a separate bowl of the boiled baby new potatoes and/or the salad.

The Ultimate Tuna Mayonnaise
with Baked Potatoes

This all-time favourite is the perfect store cupboard standby. Replace the spring onions with a couple of tablespoons of diced red or white onion, or even chives work well.

Ingredients (Serves 4)

- 4 large baking potatoes, scrubbed (each about 275g (10oz))
- 6 tbsp mayonnaise
- 4 spring onions, finely chopped
- 1 tsp Dijon mustard
- 1 tsp creamed horseradish (from a jar)
- ½ lemon, pips removed
- 400g can tuna in oil, drained
- 50g (2oz) butter
- Maldon sea salt and freshly ground black pepper
- lightly dressed mixed salad, to serve

Method

Preheat the oven to 200°C (400°F), Gas mark 6. Cut a criss-cross on the top of each potato and place directly on the oven shelf. Bake for 1 ¼ hours or until cooked through and tender.

Meanwhile, place the mayonnaise in a bowl and beat in the spring onions, mustard, horseradish and a squeeze of lemon juice. Season to taste and gently fold in the tuna.

Place each jacket potato on a warmed serving plate and cut right through the criss-cross on each one. Then using a clean tea towel, gently push the edges together to fluff up. Add a knob of butter to each one and then divide the tuna mayonnaise among them. Add some salad to each plate to serve.

Baked Sea Bass with Tomatoes and Olives

In the restaurant, I use wild sea bass, which I get from a French supplier. Wild sea bass is very expensive, but for this dish you can go to any good fishmonger, and chances are they will have a plentiful supply of farmed sea bass. It is great value for money, with a good flavour. This is a really glamorous and colourful dish that would work just as well with grey mullet.

Ingredients (Serves 4)

- 4 x 350g (12oz) whole sea bass, gutted and scaled
- 8 fresh bay leaves
- 4 tbsp rapeseed oil, plus extra for greasing
- 2 firm tomatoes, thinly sliced
- 1 lime, sliced
- 75g (3oz) black pitted olives, sliced
- 4 garlic cloves, thinly sliced
- 2 tbsp roughly chopped fresh dill
- handful fresh basil leaves
- boiled baby new potatoes and lightly dressed green salad, to serve

Method

Preheat the oven to 190°C (375°F), Gas mark 5. Using a sharp knife, cut the heads and tails off the sea bass (or get your fishmonger to do this for you), then make two slashes on each sea bass down to the bone and stud each incision with a bay leaf.

Place the sea bass on a lightly oiled roasting tin. Season the fish cavities; fill each one with the tomatoes, half of the lime slices, the olives, garlic, dill and basil leaves. Drizzle over the oil and season the fish all over again.

Roast the sea bass for 15-20 minutes, until the skin is crisp and the flesh is just cooked through and tender. When the fish is cooked, the flesh will feel firmer and the dorsal fin (the large one on the back) will pull away easily. Allow the fish to rest for 2-3 minutes, then transfer to warmed serving plates. Arrange the remaining slices of lime on the fish and serve with separate bowls of baby new potatoes and salad.

Roast Cod with Spring Vegetables

Spring vegetables taste wonderful if just simply steamed as in this recipe. Melted butter and a little seasoning to finish them off and they are perfect with the roast cod. For the best results, choose cod fillets from the centre cut and always ask the fish counter or fishmonger to ensure that all the skin and bones have been removed. You could try adding a little finely grated lemon rind and/or a crushed garlic clove to the fish fillets before drizzling with the rapeseed oil and roasting. This recipe will also work well with haddock, whiting, hake or trout fillets.

Ingredients (Serves 4)

- 4 x 175g (6oz) cod fillets, skinned and boned (from a sustainable source)
- 1 tbsp rapeseed oil

For the Spring Vegetables:
- 12 asparagus spears, peeled and trimmed
- 1 carrot, peeled and cut into small cubes
- 100g (4oz) spinach, washed and thick stalks removed
- 100g (4oz) broad beans, blanched and skinned
- 50g (2oz) butter
- 1 tsp caster sugar
- Maldon sea salt and freshly ground black pepper
- lemon wedges, to garnish

Method

Preheat the oven to 200°C (400°F), Gas mark 6. Arrange the cod fillets on a non-stick baking sheet and season, then drizzle over the oil. Roast in the oven for 8-10 minutes until cooked through and tender. This will depend on the thickness of the fillets.

To prepare the spring vegetables, steam the asparagus, carrot cubes, spinach and broad beans until just cooked through and tender. Allow them to cool slightly.

Heat the butter in a large heavy-based frying pan. Sprinkle over the sugar and then tip in the steamed vegetables, tossing until evenly combined. Season to taste. Divide the spring vegetables among warmed wide-rimmed serving bowls and place a piece of roasted cod on top of each one. Garnish with lemon wedges to serve.

Spaghetti with Dublin Bay Prawns

Dublin Bay prawns actually look a lot like small slender lobsters, with rather more delicate colouring and lighter claws in relation to the body. They may seem like an expensive luxury but are well worth every cent. At their best from late spring to late autumn, they need very little effort to make a stunning meal.

Ingredients (Serves 4)

- 20 large Dublin Bay prawns
- 350g (12oz) spaghetti
- 2 tbsp rapeseed oil
- 50g (2oz) butter, diced
- 1 red chilli, halved, seeded and cut into rings (optional)
- 2 large garlic clove, crushed
- ½ lemon, pips removed
- 1 tbsp chopped fresh flat-leaf parsley
- Maldon sea salt and freshly ground black pepper
- lightly dressed green salad and crusty bread, to serve

Method

To prepare the prawns, firmly twist the head away from the body and discard, or use for stock. Turn each prawn over and crack open the hard shell along the belly, then carefully peel it away from the flesh, twisting off the tail.

To remove the intestinal tract, which looks like a thin black vein running down the back of the prawn flesh, run the tip of a small knife down the back of each prawn and then lift up and pull out the vein. If you are lucky sometimes the vein comes away with the prawn tail or can be easily pulled out without having to cut the prawn at all.

Plunge the spaghetti into a pan of boiling salted water and cook for 8-10 minutes until 'al dente' - tender but still with a little bite.

Meanwhile, heat the oil in a large frying pan with the knob of butter. Once the butter has stopped sizzling add the chilli, if using and the garlic and sauté for about 30 seconds until the garlic is lightly golden. Tip in the prepared prawns and sauté for another few minutes until tender. The prawns will change in colour and begin to curl into a prawn shape. Be careful not to overcook. Add a good squeeze of lemon juice and sprinkle over the parsley. Add the rest of the butter, tossing to coat. Season to taste and remove from the heat.

Drain the spaghetti and return to the pan, then tip in the prawn mixture tossing to coat. Divide among warmed serving plates. Serve at once with a nice green salad and plenty of crusty bread.

Warm Crab and Spinach Tart

This recipe is for a standard tart. We do a spinach and goat's cheese tart on the Sunday lunch menu in the restaurant and it goes down well. Tarts are very much in fashion at the moment and seem to have taken over from quiches. You can make the pastry case for this tart up to 24 hours in advance, but if you're short on time, you can always use shop-bought pastry or even a ready-made pastry case instead. When I go to the trouble of making pastry, I normally make double the quantity I need and freeze the remainder to use another day.

Ingredients (Serves 4)

- knob of butter
- 350g (12oz) spinach leaves, washed and tough stalks removed
- 150ml (¼ pint) cream
- 150ml (¼ pint) milk
- 2 tbsp sweet chilli sauce (Thai Gold)
- 2 eggs, plus 2 egg yolks
- 1 tbsp snipped fresh chives
- 200g (7oz) fresh white crabmeat
- 100g (4oz) freshly grated Parmesan

For the Pastry:
- 225g (8oz) plain flour, plus extra for dusting
- 100g (4oz) butter, diced and chilled
- pinch dried chilli flakes
- 3 tbsp ice-cold water
- a little egg wash, for brushing
- Maldon sea salt and freshly ground black pepper
- lightly dressed green salad, to serve

Method

Preheat oven to 200°C (400°F), Gas mark 6. To make the pastry, place the flour, butter and chilli flakes in a food processor. Add half a teaspoon of salt and whizz briefly until the mixture forms fine crumbs. Pour in the water through the feeder tube and pulse again so that the pastry comes together. Knead gently on a lightly floured surface for a few seconds to give a smooth dough. Wrap in clingfilm and chill for at least 10 minutes before rolling (or up to an hour if time allows).

Roll out the pastry on a lightly floured surface and use to line a loose-bottomed 21cm (8½in) fluted flan tin that is about 4cm (1½in) deep. Use a rolling pin to lift the pastry into the tin, pressing well into sides and letting the pastry overhang a little as this prevents shrinkage. Chill for another 10 minutes to let the pastry rest. Prick the pastry base with a fork, then line with a circle of oiled foil or parchment paper that is first crumpled up to make it easier to handle. Fill with baking beans or dried pulses and bake for 10 minutes until the pastry case looks set, but not coloured.

Carefully remove the foil or paper and lower the temperature to 160°C (325°F), Gas mark 3, then brush with the egg wash to form a seal. Return to the oven for another 5 minutes or until the base is firm to the touch and the sides are lightly coloured.

Heat the butter in a small pan and tip in the spinach. Sauté for a minute until wilted, then season to taste. Leave the spinach until cool enough to handle, then squeeze dry and finely chop.

Beat together the cream in a bowl with the milk, chilli sauce, eggs and egg yolks until well combined. Stir in the chives and season to taste. Scatter the finely chopped spinach and crabmeat in the bottom of the pastry case and sprinkle the Parmesan on top, then pour in the cream mixture and bake for about 25 minutes until the filling is just set but still slightly wobbly in the middle. Leave to rest for 5 minutes in the tin, then remove and trim down the excess pastry. To serve, while still warm, carefully cut the crab and spinach tart into slices. Arrange on serving plates with the salad.

Fragrant Prawn Curry and Coconut Curry

This prawn and coconut curry has eating and drinking in it, as they say in Cavan. Be careful to put the prawns in at the last minute, as you just want to warm them through. This recipe is also delicious with thinly sliced chicken or even beef instead of the prawns.

Ingredients (Serves 4)

- 2 potatoes, diced
- 1 tbsp sunflower oil
- 1 onion, thinly sliced
- 1 garlic clove, crushed
- 1 tsp freshly grated root ginger
- 1 tbsp medium curry powder
- 1 tsp tomato purée
- 300ml (½ pint) vegetable stock (see Essentials page 213)
- 40og can coconut milk
- 450g (1lb) raw tiger prawns, peeled with tails left on
- 175g (6oz) green beans, trimmed and halved
- 50g (2oz) toasted coconut flakes
- salt and freshly ground pepper
- Thai fragrant rice, to serve
- natural yoghurt and sliced spring onion, to garnish

Method

Cook the potatoes in a pan of boiling salted water for 10-12 minutes or until tender, then drain.

Heat the oil in a large pan. Add the onion, garlic and ginger and sauté for 5 minutes until tender. Add the curry powder and cook for 2 minutes. Add the tomato purée, vegetable stock and coconut milk and bring to the boil, then reduce the heat and simmer for 10 minutes until slightly reduced and thickened, stirring occasionally.

Add the cooked potatoes with the green beans and prawns and cook for another few minutes until the prawns are tender and the beans still have a little bite. Season to taste. Ladle the curry into warmed serving bowls on top of some rice. Top each one with a swirl of natural yoghurt, sliced spring onion and toasted coconut flakes to serve.

Vegetarian and Vegetable Side Orders

Spicy Chickpea and Sweet Potato Curry

The spicy chickpea recipe is a vegetarian option which I got from my good friend Nazanne Booth in Enniskillen. She is a fantastic cook and made the wedding cake when Amelda and I got married. And while this is the veggie version, you can add according to your tastes. I particularly like this with prawns. And, once again, it does improve if made the day before.

Ingredients (Serves 4)

- 2 tbsp rapeseed oil
- 1 small onion, thinly sliced
- 450g (1lb) sweet potatoes
- 2 garlic cloves, crushed
- 1 tsp finely chopped fresh root ginger
- 1 green chilli, seeded and finely chopped (optional)
- 1 tsp garam masala
- 1 tsp mild chilli powder
- 1 tsp ground turmeric
- 400g can chopped tomatoes
- 300ml (½ pint) vegetable stock (see Essentials page 213)
- 400g can chickpeas, drained and rinsed
- 175g (6oz) spinach
- Maldon sea salt and freshly ground black pepper
- steamed basmati rice, to serve
- fresh coriander leaves, to garnish

Method

Peel the sweet potatoes and cut into 1cm (½in) slices. Heat the oil in a large pan and add the sweet potatoes. Cook for 2-3 minutes until just beginning to colour, turning once. Remove from the pan and place in a bowl. Set aside.

Add the onion to the pan and sauté for 2-3 minutes until softened and then add the garlic, ginger and chilli, if using, and cook for a minute or two, stirring. Add the garam masala to the pan with the chilli powder and ground turmeric and cook for another minute, stirring continuously.

Add the tomatoes to the onion and spice mixture, stirring to combine and bring to a gentle simmer. Cook for 15-20 minutes until well reduced and thickened, stirring occasionally to prevent the bottom sticking. Pour the stock into the pan and then add the chickpeas and reserved sweet potato slices, stirring to combine. Simmer gently for another 30 minutes or until the liquid has reduced to a sauce consistency.

Wash the spinach and remove any tough stalks, then once the sauce has achieved the correct consistency, add to the pan and allow to just wilt down. Season to taste.

To serve, spoon the chickpea and sweet potato curry into warmed bowls and garnish with the coriander. Place a separate bowl of the rice on the table and allow people to help themselves.

Back Garden Salad with Tomato and Herb Pesto

This is the year we embraced gardening, starting with one poly tunnel. To be honest, most of the work is being done by Amelda's uncle Gerry Baxter, but we have all been getting a great deal of pleasure from it. The food you grow yourself always tastes the best. We have lots of courgettes and are growing a variety of beans so this recipe was devised to use up what we have. Feel free to experiment with your own selection of home grown vegetables!

Ingredients (Serves 4)

- 150g (5oz) runner beans
- 100g (4oz) shelled broad beans
- 4 spring onions, thinly sliced
- 1 tbsp rapeseed oil
- knob of butter
- 1 large red pepper, seeded and thinly sliced
- 2 medium courgettes, peeled and cut into long strips
- handful fresh basil leaves, roughly torn
- handful fresh coriander leaves

For the Pesto:
- 100g (4oz) of semi sun-dried or sun blush tomatoes, drained
- 8 basil leaves
- small handful fresh flat-leaf parsley leaves
- 1 garlic clove, peeled
- pinch mild chilli powder
- 50g (2oz) freshly grated Parmesan
- 175ml (6fl oz) rapeseed oil
- Maldon sea salt and freshly ground black pepper

Method

To make the tomato and herb pesto, place the tomatoes and herbs in a food processor with the garlic, chilli powder, Parmesan and a quarter of the oil. Blend to a paste, and then slowly add the remaining oil. Transfer to a bowl and season to taste. Cover with clingfilm and chill until needed.

Trim the runner beans and then cut them into long, thin strips. Cook them briefly in boiling salted water until just tender, then cool quickly by placing into cold water.

Blanch the shelled broad beans in boiling water for 1 minute. Drain into a sieve and hold under running cold water to cool them down quickly. Drain again and peel off the outer hard skins – make a nick in the tops and pop the beans out. Set aside until needed.

Just before assembling, heat a large frying pan with the oil and butter. Briefly stir-fry the red peppers until beginning to soften.

Add the blanched runner and broad beans, toss to warm through, then tip out onto a warmed serving platter and season to taste. Keep warm.

Finally, gently fry the courgette strips for a few minutes each side until golden and softened. Scatter over the vegetables with the spring onions, basil and coriander leaves. Spoon over the tomato and herb pesto to serve.

Chargrilled Vegetable Layered Sandwich with Tapanade

For the chargrilled vegetable layered sandwich, begin preparations the day before you want to eat it. You can add almost any flavours to this kind of layered-up loaf. Experiment with basil pesto (see Essentials page 193) instead of the tapenade, or add a layer of spinach, watercress, different cheeses, smoked salmon or even fresh white crabmeat. All would work well with the grilled vegetables.

Ingredients (Serves 4-6)

- 150ml (1/4 pint) rapeseed oil
- 2 garlic cloves, crushed
- 4 dried small red chillies, roughly chopped
- 1 tbsp chopped fresh flat-leaf parsley
- 2 red peppers, cut into quarters and seeds removed
- 2 yellow peppers, cut into quarters and seeds removed
- 2 small courgettes, thinly sliced lengthways
- 2 small red onions, sliced into thick rounds
- 1 aubergine, cut into 1cm (½in) rounds
- 1 rustic round loaf, measuring about 25cm (10in) across
- 4 tbsp tapenade (from a jar)
- 1 small bunch fresh basil leaves finely shredded
- 2 x 100g (4oz) balls mozzarella, very thinly sliced
- 40g (1½oz) wild rocket
- Maldon sea salt and freshly ground black pepper

Method

Place the oil in a shallow non-metallic dish and stir in the garlic, chillies and parsley and then season to taste. Add the peppers, courgettes and onions and leave to marinate at room temperature for one hour if time allows. Toss the aubergines in the marinade at the last minute so that they don't absorb too much of the oil. Arrange the vegetables on a heated griddle pan (or the grill rack over medium-hot coals of a barbecue) and cook for 6-8 minutes until completely softened and richly coloured, turning regularly and lightly basting with any remaining marinade.

Meanwhile, cut a 1cm (½in) slice off the top of the loaf. Hollow out the bread with your fingers (make breadcrumbs with the torn out bread for use in another recipe) to leave a case with walls about 1cm (½in) thick. Spread three tablespoons of the tapenade all around the inside and the remaining tablespoon on the lid underside.

As soon as the vegetables are cooked, remove them from the heat and layer them up inside the loaf, sprinkling each layer with basil and seasoning to taste. I would start with the aubergine, then the sliced mozzarella, the red peppers, yellow peppers, onions and courgettes. Top with the rocket, pressing it down gently.

Replace the top of the loaf and wrap the whole thing tightly with a couple of layers of clingfilm. Place the filled loaf in the fridge overnight with something heavy sitting on top like a wooden board or a tray with unopened cans on top. Take on a picnic, allowing the whole thing to come back to room temperature, then unwrap and cut into thick wedges to serve with plenty of paper napkins.

Pumpkin and Basil Macaroni

When you're in the mood for a real winter warmer that has loads of flavour, appeals to all the family and doesn't take too long to prepare, you can't go far wrong with this pasta bake. It can be made in advance but just might take a little longer to reheat in the oven. I like to serve it with a nice fresh green salad or some steamed purple sprouting broccoli.

Ingredients (Serves 4)

- 350g (12oz) cherry tomatoes on the vine
- 450g (1lb) pumpkin, peeled, seeded and diced
- 2 garlic cloves, finely chopped
- 2 tbsp rapeseed oil
- 350g (12oz) macaroni pasta
- 250g carton mascarpone cheese
- 2 tsp Dijon mustard
- 2 tbsp fresh basil leaves, shredded, plus extra leaves to garnish
- 200g (/oz) freshly grated Parmesan cheese
- Maldon sea salt and freshly ground black pepper

Method

Preheat oven 220°C (425°F), Gas mark 7. Carefully remove the cherry tomatoes from the vine and place in an ovenproof dish alongside the diced pumpkin. Sprinkle with half the garlic and drizzle over the oil. Season to taste. Roast for 15 minutes until the tomatoes have softened slightly and skins have started to split, tossing once or twice to ensure even cooking.

Meanwhile, cook the macaroni in a large pan of boiling salted water for 8-10 minutes, or according to packet instructions until 'al dente' - tender but firm to the bite.

Place the mascarpone in a bowl and beat in the mustard, basil, Parmesan and the remaining garlic. Drain the pasta and return to the pan. Stir in the mascarpone cheese mixture, then carefully fold in the roasted cherry tomatoes and pumpkin. Season to taste.

Tip into the ovenproof dish that you used for the tomatoes and pumpkin. Bake for 20 minutes until bubbling and golden brown. To serve, leave the cheese, tomato and basil macaroni to stand for a few minutes, then garnish with basil leaves and serve straight from the dish onto warmed serving plates.

Quick Quesadillas with Chilli Salsa and Sour Cream

I have a Mexican chef, Maritinez, working with me now and he has taught me a lot about Mexican food. These quesadillas are a perfect lunch or mid-morning snack for all of the family to enjoy. They can be prepared up to one hour in advance, covered with clingfilm and kept at room temperature. Simply flash through the oven when you are ready to serve. The salsa is also good with simple grilled fish – like cod, hake or haddock – or some grilled goat's cheese.

Ingredients (Serves 4)

- 8 soft flour tortillas
- 2 tbsp rapeseed oil, plus extra for brushing
- 225g (8oz) Cheddar cheese, grated
- 1 mild red chilli, seeded and finely chopped
- 4 spring onions, finely chopped
- about 120ml (4fl oz) sour cream

For the Chilli Salsa:

- 2 medium vine ripened tomatoes, seeded and diced
- 1 small red onion, diced
- 2 tbsp chopped fresh coriander, plus extra leaves to garnish
- 1 mild red chilli, seeded and finely chopped
- juice of ½ lime
- 2 tbsp extra-virgin rapeseed oil
- Maldon sea salt and freshly ground black pepper

Method

To make the chilli salsa, place the tomatoes in a non-metallic bowl with the red onion, coriander, chilli, lime juice and oil, stirring until well combined. Season to taste, cover with clingfilm and leave at room temperature to allow the flavours to develop.

Preheat the oven to 200°C (400°F), Gas mark 6 and heat a griddle pan over a medium heat until very hot. Brush one side of each tortilla with a little oil. Place one tortilla in the pan, oiled-side down, and cook for one minute until nicely marked, pressing down with a spatula. Repeat with remaining tortillas.

Arrange half the tortillas on baking sheets, marked-side down. Sprinkle over the cheese and then scatter the chilli and spring onions on top. Season to taste. Cover with the remaining tortillas, marked-side up, and bake for about 5 minutes or until heated through and the cheese has melted. Allow to cool slightly until easy to handle.

Cut each quesadilla into eight wedges with a serrated knife, pizza cutter or kitchen scissors. Garnish each wedge with a small spoonful of sour cream and a coriander leaf. Arrange on warmed serving plates and place small bowls of the chilli salsa to the side of each one to serve.

Spicy Vegetable and Cashew Noodles

This is a tasty noodle dish that you will find very easy to make. Some people are not keen on aubergines – or eggplant, as it is known in America. I enjoy it, but leave it out if it's not to your taste. Instead of snap peas, you could use mange tout or green beans.

Ingredients (Serves 4)

- 4 tbsp rapeseed oil
- 2 small aubergines, trimmed and cut into small chunks
- 2 red peppers, seeded and cut into strips
- 100g (4oz) chestnut mushrooms, sliced
- 100g (4oz) sugar snap peas
- 2 garlic cloves, crushed
- 1 small red chilli, seeded and finely chopped
- 2.5cm (1in) piece root ginger, peeled and finely chopped
- 2 tbsp light soy sauce (Thai Gold)
- 1 tsp light brown sugar
- 500ml (18fl oz) vegetable stock (see Essentials page 213)
- 450g (1lb) wholemeal ramen noodles
- 75g (3oz) toasted cashew nuts
- 2 tbsp freshly chopped coriander

Method

Heat the oil in a wok or large frying pan. Add the aubergines and peppers and stir fry for 3-4 minutes, then tip in the sugar snap peas and mushrooms and stir fry for another 2-3 minutes until the vegetables are just tender.

Tip the garlic, chilli and ginger into the wok and stir fry for a minute or two, then add the soy sauce, sugar and stock and simmer for a further 5 minutes until slightly reduced and all the vegetables are completely tender.

Meanwhile, cook the noodles according to the packet instructions. Drain the noodles and divide between warmed deep serving bowls. Spoon over the spicy vegetable mixture and scatter over the cashew nuts and coriander to serve.

Baked Mediterranean Vegetables with Tomato and Cooleeney Cheese

This is a wonderfully light Mediterranean dish inspired by something I had whilst on holiday in Italy. Aubergines, which some of you know as eggplant, are under-used in my view. And instead of Parmesan you could use a good hard Irish cheese if you like. Irish cheese has come on in leaps and bounds and now there is such a variety to choose from.

Ingredients (Serves 4)

- 5 tbsp extra-virgin rapeseed oil
- 1 red onion, cut into cubes
- 1 large red pepper, halved, seeded and cut into cubes
- 1 garlic clove, crushed
- 1 large aubergine, cut into cubes
- 450g (1lb) vine tomatoes
- 450g (1lb) small courgettes
- 1 tsp chopped fresh thyme
- 1 tbsp chopped fresh basil
- 175g (6oz) Cooleeney cheese, sliced
- 2 tbsp fresh white breadcrumbs
- 2 tbsp freshly grated Parmesan
- Maldon sea salt and freshly ground black pepper
- lightly dressed green salad
- crusty bread, to serve

Method

Preheat oven to 180°C (350°F), Gas mark 4. Heat two tablespoons of the oil in a large frying pan. Add the red onion and sauté for a couple of minutes until lightly browned. Add the red pepper, garlic and aubergine, then season to taste and cook over a low heat for 12-15 minutes until softened, stirring occasionally.

When cooked, scatter the sautéed vegetables in the bottom of an ovenproof dish. Cut the tomatoes and courgettes into thick rounds and then arrange in overlapping rows on top of the sautéed vegetables. Tuck in the slices of Cooley cheese and sprinkle over the thyme and basil. Season generously, then drizzle over the remaining oil and bake for 30 minutes until all of the vegetables are just cooked through and tender and the cheese is bubbling.

Remove the dish from the oven and sprinkle over the breadcrumbs and Parmesan, then return to oven for 10 minutes to form a light crust. Serve straight to the table with bowls of the green salad and bread.

Grilled Asparagus with Red Peppers, Parmesan and Balsamic Reduction

This balsamic reduction is what I think of as a store cupboard essential. It is great over roasted vegetables or cooked meats. Instead of Parmesan you might like to try Cooley which is a good hard Irish cheese. Alternatively to make this a more substantial meal you could add some Boilie goat's cheese balls which have great flavour and do not taste too strong.

Ingredients (Serves 4)

- 2 bunches asparagus
- 4 tbsp extra-virgin rapeseed oil
- 6 fresh basil leaves, torn, plus extra to garnish
- 3 fresh thyme sprigs, plus extra to garnish
- 1 tbsp chopped fresh flat-leaf parsley
- 3 large red peppers
- 4 garlic cloves, unpeeled
- 300ml (½ pint) balsamic vinegar
- 50g (2oz) toasted pine nuts
- 75g (3oz) Parmesan cheese shavings
- 25g (1oz) wild rocket
- Maldon sea salt and freshly ground black pepper
- crusty bread, to serve

Method

To prepare the asparagus spears, trim about 5cm (2in) of the woody ends from each spear. Bring a large pan of salted water to the boil and blanch the asparagus tips for 2 minutes, then drain and quickly refresh in a bowl of iced cold water. Drain again and dry thoroughly, then place in a non-metallic dish.

Add two tablespoons of the oil to the asparagus with the basil, thyme and parsley, turning to coat them evenly. Season to taste, then cover with clingfilm and leave to marinade for one hour or overnight in the fridge is fine.

Preheat the oven to 200°C (400°F), Gas mark 6. Place red peppers in a roasting tin with the garlic and drizzle over the remaining oil. Roast for 30-40 minutes until skins are well charred and the peppers are completely tender. Remove from the oven and carefully place the peppers in polythene bag. Tie securely and leave to cool completely. The steam will help remove the skin easily. Once the peppers are cool, remove from the bag and cut each pepper in half, then discard the cores and seeds and set aside until needed.

Peel the garlic cloves and then mash the flesh to a paste. Stir into the marinating asparagus mixture. To make balsamic reduction, place the balsamic vinegar in a heavy-based pan and bring to the boil. Simmer for 15-20 minutes until you have achieved a syrup-like consistency, stirring occasionally. Leave to cool and then transfer to a plastic squeezy bottle. This will keep happily in the fridge for up to three months.

When ready to serve, heat a griddle pan until very hot. Add the roasted peppers to the asparagus mixture, tossing to coat in the marinade, then carefully arrange the asparagus and peppers on the griddle pan and cook for 3 minutes until lightly charred and heated through, turning once. You may have to do this in batches depending on the size of your griddle pan.

To serve, arrange the peppers and asparagus spears on warmed serving plates. Scatter over the toasted pine nuts and drizzle around some of the balsamic syrup. Finally scatter over the Parmesan shavings, basil leaves and thyme. Serve with a separate basket of the crusty bread.

Italian Bean Salad with Griddled Red Onion

Good quality ingredients are needed for this Italian bean salad which should be served at room temperature. It makes excellent picnic food, or can be used as an addition to an antipasti platter or as a fairly instant lunch. You can also use haricot or borlotti beans. Stirring the beans into freshly cooked pasta makes a very healthy, wholesome meal for the family. If you don't have a griddle pan, you should go out and get a good cast-iron one. No kitchen should be without one as they are so useful.

Ingredients (Serves 4)

- 2 red onions, cut into wedges but root left intact
- 120ml (4fl oz) extra-virgin rapeseed oil
- juice of ½ lemon
- pinch sugar
- 2 x 400g cans cannellini beans, drained and rinsed
- 15g (½oz) fresh flat-leaf parsley, stalks removed and roughly chopped
- Maldon sea salt and freshly ground black pepper

Method

Preheat a griddle pan. Toss the onion wedges in a bowl with two tablespoons of the oil and season generously. Add to the griddle pan and cook for 6-8 minutes until cooked through and lightly charred, turning occasionally.

Meanwhile, prepare the dressing. Place the remaining oil in a screw-topped jar with the lemon juice, sugar and season to taste. Shake until well combined and pour into a serving dish.

When the onions are cooked through, add them to the dressing, turning gently to combine, then gently fold in the beans and parsley. Season to taste and leave at room temperature for about one hour to allow the flavours to combine if time allows before serving.

Parsnip, Shallot and Potato Cakes

These parsnip, shallot and potato cakes go very well with a steak. Or you can use them on their own as a starter topped with a poached egg. They can be prepared well in advance and if you cannot get shallots, use red onions instead. To my mind, parsnip is a much-undervalued vegetable and has the most fantastic flavour when prepared correctly. If your specimens are large, remove the woody core before cutting them into chunks.

Ingredients (Serves 4)

- 450g (1lb) parsnips, cut into chunks
- 450g (1lb) potatoes, cut into chunks
- 4 tbsp rapeseed oil
- 4 shallots, cut into thin wedges but root left intact
- 1 tbsp chopped fresh sage or flat-leaf parsley
- 50g (2oz) plain flour
- knob of butter
- Maldon sea salt and freshly ground black pepper

Method

Cook the potatoes and parsnips in a large pan of boiling water for 15-20 minutes or until tender. Drain and mash until smooth, then season to taste.

Meanwhile, heat two tablespoons of the oil in a large frying pan and sauté the shallots for 5 minutes until softened but not coloured.

Beat the shallot mixture into the mashed parsnips and potatoes with the herbs, then season to taste. Shape into eight rounds, pressing the mixture firmly together.

Place the four on a flat plate and season generously, then use to dust the patties, shaking off any excess.

Add the remaining oil and butter to the large frying pan over a medium heat and once the butter is foaming, add the patties. Cook for 2-3 minutes on each side or until crisp and golden brown. Arrange on warmed serving plates to serve.

Colcannon

This is my standard colcannon recipe which, once mastered, can be adapted for different results. Try replacing the milk with crème fraîche or use a carton of quark (skimmed milk soft cheese). Jane Cassidy from Kilbeg in Kells, Co. Meath produces wonderful quark, as well as many other excellent dairy products. I also like adding some snipped fresh chives or a good dollop of Dijon mustard, depending on what I plan to serve it with.

Ingredients (Serves 4)

- 675g (1½lb) floury potatoes, scrubbed (as even-sized as possible)
- ½ Savoy cabbage, cored and thinly shredded
- 100ml (3½fl oz) milk
- 50g (2oz) butter
- 2 spring onions, finely chopped
- Maldon sea salt and freshly ground white pepper

Method

Place the unpeeled potatoes in a pan of salted water and bring to the boil. Reduce the heat and simmer for 20-25 minutes or until tender. Drain and return to the pan, then cover with a tea towel for 5 minutes to dry off. Leave to cool slightly.

Meanwhile, blanch the shredded cabbage in a separate pan of boiling, salted water for 2-3 minutes until tender but still crisp. Drain well and refresh under cold running water.

Pour the milk into a small pan and add the butter and spring onions. Warm gently for a few minutes without boiling as you want the spring onions to remain crunchy.

Peel the cooked potatoes and mash well, (using a potato ricer if you have one) and put into a clean pan. Gradually pour in the warm milk mixture, beating continuously with a wooden spoon to combine. Fold in the cabbage and then gently reheat, stirring constantly. Season to taste. To serve, place the colcannon in a warmed serving bowl and bring straight to the table.

Desserts

Baked Lemon and Vanilla Cheesecake

For a treat, it is hard to beat this baked lemon and vanilla cheesecake. It is easy to make and everybody loves it. I use the soft cheeses made by Jane and Kieran Cassidy at Kilbeg Dairies in Co. Meath. It is one of the most beautiful dairies I have ever visited. They were the first in Ireland to make quark, which is a German-style cream cheese that is very low in fat.

Ingredients (Serves 8-10)

For the Base:
- 75g (3oz) butter, plus a little extra for greasing
- 225g (8oz) digestive biscuits, finely crushed

For the Topping:
- 75g (3oz) sultanas
- 1 tbsp dark rum
- 450g (1lb) soft cream cheese
- 250g (9oz) sour cream or quark
- 150g (5oz) caster sugar
- 4 eggs, separated
- 50g (2oz) plain flour
- 1 vanilla pod, seeds scraped out
- finely grated rind and juice of 2 lemons
- icing sugar and finely pared rind of lemon, to decorate
- lightly whipped cream, to serve

Method

To prepare the topping, place the sultanas in a non-metallic dish with the rum and set aside for one hour to plump up.

Preheat the oven to 160°C (325°F), Gas mark 3. To make the base of the cheesecake, grease a 23cm (9in) loose-bottomed cake tin.

To make the base, melt the butter in a pan over a gentle heat. Add the crushed biscuits and mix well to combine. Spread the mixture evenly over the base of the tin, pressing down with the back of a spoon to flatten into the corners. Chill for 10-15 minutes to firm up.

Meanwhile, finish making the filling. Place the soft cream cheese, sour cream or quark, caster sugar, egg yolks, plain flour, vanilla seeds, lemon rind and juice in a bowl. Beat together with an electric whisk until smooth and well combined. In a separate bowl, whisk the egg whites until stiff peaks form. Using a large metal spoon, carefully fold the whites into the soft cheese mixture until just combined. Gently fold in the soaked sultanas.

Carefully pour the soft cheese mixture into the tin on top of the biscuit base. Using a palette knife, spread out evenly to cover the base completely. Bake for 60-70 minutes until golden brown and just set. It should be slightly wobbly in the middle. Turn off the oven and leave the cheesecake to cool in the oven. Once cooled, carefully remove from the tin and transfer to a serving plate. Dust with icing sugar and scatter over the pared lemon rind just before serving. Cut into slices and arrange on serving plates with cream.

Chocolate Fondue

Make sure you get good quality plain chocolate (richer and creamier than eating chocolate, with a very high cocoa butter content). Green & Black is excellent, as is Lindt. I have used cherries in this recipe instead of strawberries at times, and I love plums when they're in season. Tradition states that, as you drop your fruit into the fondue, you must kiss the person opposite you – so be careful who you invite! If you want to serve this individually, skewer a mixture of fruits for each person and serve with a small dish of the chocolate fondue on each plate.

Ingredients (Serves 4-6)

- 300ml (½ pint) cream
- 50ml (2fl oz) milk
- 1 vanilla pod
- 450g (1lb) plain chocolate, finely chopped (at least 55% cocoa solids)
- 1 banana
- 3 apples
- 1 small pineapple
- 150g (5oz) strawberries
- 100g (4oz) marshmallows
- 50g (2oz) sponge fingers

Method

Place the cream and milk in a small pan. Using a sharp knife, split the vanilla pod in half lengthways and then using the back of the knife scrape the seeds into the pan. Slowly heat until just at boiling point. Remove from the heat and stir in the chocolate until melted. Keep the fondue warm by sitting the pan within a larger pan of hand-hot water.

Cut the fruit into large slices or chunks, depending on the type of fruit. Leave the strawberries whole. To serve, transfer the fondue to a heatproof serving bowl and place in the centre of the table with the fruit, marshmallows and sponge fingers arranged in small dishes around it. Then allow each person to dip one piece of fruit or marshmallow at a time into the fondue.

Chocolate Tart

This chocolate tart is also delicious served slightly warm with some good-quality ice cream and fresh raspberries. And here is a good tip: blind bake by covering the pastry with tin foil, then add baking beans to stop the pastry from rising. When it is cooked, you may brush it with egg wash, as this will seal the base and prevent the filling from sticking to the bottom of the tin.

Ingredients (Serves 6-8)

For the Pastry:
- 100g (4oz) butter, diced
- 175g (6oz) plain flour, plus extra for dusting
- pinch salt
- 50g (2oz) caster sugar
- 1 egg yolk
- ½ tbsp cream

For the Filling:
- 450g (1lb) plain chocolate, broken into squares (at least 55% cocoa solids)
- 1 tsp cocoa powder
- 4 eggs
- 75g (3oz) caster sugar
- 300ml (½ pint) cream
- 150ml (¼ pint) milk
- crème fraîche and redcurrant sprigs, to serve

Method

Preheat the oven to 180°C (350°F), Gas mark 4. To make the pastry, place the butter, flour, salt and sugar in a food mixer and blend. Add the yolk and cream and mix together until just combined. Do not over-work or the pastry will be tough. Cover in clingfilm. Chill for one hour. Roll out the pastry on a lightly floured work surface and use to line a 23cm (9in) loose-bottomed flan tin and blind bake for about 20 minutes or until cooked through and golden brown.

Reduce the oven temperature to 130°C (260°F), Gas mark ¾ and make the filling. Place the chocolate, cocoa powder, eggs and sugar in a bowl. Boil cream and milk together in a heavy-based pan. Pour the hot milk-cream mix over the chocolate mixture and whisk until smooth, then pass through a sieve into a jug.

Carefully pour the filling into the prepared pastry case until almost full. If you have remaining filling it will keep for up to one week in the fridge. Bake for 30-40 minutes until the tart is cooked through but there is still a slight wobble in the centre. Leave to cool to room temperature and then cut into slices and arrange on serving plates with quenelles of crème fraîche and redcurrant sprigs to serve.

Fruit and Yoghurt Pot

This fruit and yoghurt pot makes a great dessert or even breakfast. I like the fruit chopped but a bit rough and ready. You can literally throw it together, and you do not even need to use a blender. This recipe works just as well with bananas, apples and grapes. It is tasty and packed with slow-release energy foods that will keep you going throughout the day. We always use Mileeven's honey from Kilkenny in the restaurant as it has such a great flavour.

Ingredients (Serves 4)

- 100g (4oz) skinned nuts, such as hazelnuts, walnuts and/or almonds
- 500g carton low-fat natural yoghurt
- 4 tbsp runny honey
- 4 ripe bananas
- 225g (8oz) mixed berries, such as strawberries, raspberries and/or blueberries

Method

Preheat the oven to 180°C (350°F), Gas mark 4. Place the nuts in a small baking tin and roast for 6-8 minutes until toasted. Leave to cool completely and then finely chop. Set aside until needed.

Peel the bananas and cut into slices. Place in the bottom of serving glasses with the berries. Mix the yoghurt and honey together in a jug and pour over the fruit to cover completely. Cover with a layer of the chopped nuts.

Serve the fruit and yoghurt pots immediately or this keeps well covered with clingfilm overnight. Just don't sprinkle the nuts on until the last minute as they will go soggy.

Passion Fruit Mousse with Lemon Sables

This passion fruit mousse with lemon sables is the perfect way to end a special meal. It can be made well in advance and kept in the fridge until needed. These delicious biscuits are crisp, yet melt-in-the-mouth and perfect for dipping.

Ingredients (Serves 4)

For the Mousse:
- finely grated rind of 2 lemons
- 50g (2oz) caster sugar
- 3 passion fruit, halved and pulp scooped out
- 2 eggs, separated
- 40g (1½oz) butter, diced and chilled
- 8 raspberries

For the Lemon Sables:
- 50g (2oz) plain flour
- 25g (1oz) icing sugar, plus extra for dusting
- finely grated rind of 1 lemon
- 50g (2oz) butter, at room temperature
- 1 egg yolk
- grapeseed oil, for brushing

Method

To make the lemon sables, sift the flour and icing sugar into a bowl. Stir in the lemon rind and then add the butter and egg yolk. Beat well to form a soft dough. Roll out the dough between two large pieces of parchment paper to a 3mm (⅛in) thickness. Place on a large baking sheet and chill for at least 30 minutes to allow the dough to firm up.

Preheat the oven to 190°C (375°F), Gas mark 5. When ready to use, carefully peel away the top piece of parchment paper and then stamp out heart shapes or 2.5cm (1in) rounds using a biscuit cutter. Transfer to parchment lined baking sheets and bake for 8-10 minutes until crisp and lightly golden. Transfer to a wire rack and leave to cool completely, then store in an airtight tin until needed

To make the passion fruit mousse, place the lemon rind in a heatproof bowl with half of the sugar, the pulp from two passion fruit and the egg yolks. Set over a pan of simmering water and cook over a low heat for 8-10 minutes until the mixture coats the back of a spoon, stirring occasionally. Whisk in the butter, a little at a time until smooth and shiny. Remove from heat and leave to cool.

Whisk the egg whites in a separate bowl until soft peaks form, then add the remaining sugar, a bit at a time until stiff and shiny. Fold half into the cooled passion fruit mixture using a slotted spoon, then fold in the remainder. Divide among serving glasses and chill for at least two hours or overnight is fine, covered with clingfilm.

Arrange the glasses on serving plates and decorate each glass with the pulp from half a passion fruit and the raspberries. Place a couple of the lemon sables on the side for dipping to serve.

Pots of Caramel Cream with Summer Berries and Praline

This dessert is a great favourite in the restaurant, particularly after Sunday lunch. It is essential to have good quality ice cream made with fresh milk and cream. We make our own in the restaurant but around the country there are lots of farmers who have diversified and are making very high-quality ice cream so keep an eye out locally. Any leftover praline is also delicious sprinkled over a rhubarb crumble or a Pavlova.

Ingredients (Serves 4)

- 300ml (½ pint) milk
- 300ml (½ pint) cream
- 1 vanilla pod, split in half and seeds scraped out
- 175g (6oz) caster sugar
- 2 eggs, plus 4 egg yolks
- 4 scoops vanilla ice cream
- 400g (14oz) mixed berries, such as strawberries, raspberries and/or blueberries

For the Praline:
- 50g (2oz) caster sugar
- 100g (4oz) toasted skinned hazelnuts, finely chopped

Method

Preheat the oven to 150°C (300°F), Gas mark 2. Place the milk, cream and vanilla seeds in a large pan over a medium heat. Bring to boil and then set aside to infuse.

Place 100g (4oz) of the sugar in a small heavy-based pan with two tablespoons of water and cook over a medium heat. When the sugar has dissolved, let the liquid boil to a rich golden caramel colour. Remove from the heat and pour the caramel into the milk mixture – be careful as this will foam up. Return to a low heat to allow the caramel to melt back into the milk. When it has returned to the boil, it is ready.

Whisk the eggs and egg yolks with the remaining sugar in a bowl until pale in colour. Slowly pour in the caramel milk, whisking continuously. Strain through a sieve into another bowl, spooning off any froth. Carefully pour this mixture into 4 x 200ml (7fl oz) ramekins or brûlée dishes, then place in a deep roasting tin. Pour some boiling water into the tin so that it comes half way up the sides of the ramekins, minding not to touch the custard and cover the whole lot tightly with foil.

Place the caramel creams in the centre of the oven and cook for 30-40 minutes. The centre of each custard should still be slightly wobbly, as it will continue to cook when it is out of the oven. Allow to cool in the tin and then place in the fridge for at least two hours or overnight is best.

To make the praline, place the sugar and nuts into a heavy-based pan over a medium heat and caramelise gently, stirring to coat the hazelnuts. Once browned, pour the mixture out onto a non-stick baking sheet; spread out and leave to cool. Once cooled and set, smash the praline into pieces with a mallet or a rolling pin.

To serve, place the ramekins in the centre of serving plates and sprinkle praline on top. Add a scoop of ice cream to the side of each one alongside an attractive mound of the summer berries.

Sticky Toffee Pudding

Sticky toffee pudding is a classic. When I made it on TV for Home Chef, I really noticed how many people in the restaurant asked for it. It is traditionally thought of as a heavy dessert but this is a light version. I like to use the Medjool dates. They are more expensive but worth it for this dessert. I love their sticky caramel texture and taste.

Ingredients (Serves 6)

- 250g (9oz) stoned dates, roughly chopped
- 1 tsp bicarbonate of soda
- 150g (5oz) butter, at room temperature
- 175g (6oz) light brown sugar
- 175g (6oz) self-raising flour
- 2 eggs, beaten
- 1 tsp vanilla extract

For the Sauce:

- 275g (10oz) caster sugar
- 250ml (9fl oz) cream
- 75g (3oz) unsalted butter
- ½ vanilla pod, split in half and seeds scraped out
- whipped cream or vanilla ice cream, to serve

Method

Preheat the oven to 180°C (350°F), Gas mark 4. Lightly butter and line a 20cm (8in) baking tin that is at least 5cm (2in) deep with parchment paper and then set on a baking sheet. Place the dates in a pan with 300ml (½ pint) of water and bring to the boil. Then reduce the heat to a simmer and cook for about 5 minutes until the dates are soft.

Add the bicarbonate of soda to the date mixture, which will cause it to foam up and then set aside to cool a little.

Meanwhile, cream the butter and sugar together in a bowl until light and fluffy. This will take about 5 minutes.

Place the date mixture in a food processor and blend for a couple of minutes until smooth. Add one tablespoon of the flour to the butter and sugar mixture. Then slowly add the eggs and beat well to combine. Add the blended date mixture with the remaining flour and the vanilla extract and combine everything gently to give a smooth dropping consistency.

Pour the pudding batter into the prepared baking tin and bake for about 55 minutes to one hour until firm to the touch. Leave to cool a little in the tin before turning out.

Meanwhile, make the caramel sauce. Place the sugar in a pan with 150ml (¼ pint) of water. Bring to the boil and then reduce to simmer for about 15 minutes until golden brown. Stir in the cream, butter and vanilla seeds. This will seize but will eventually melt back together. Stir on a low heat to a thick consistency and keep warm. This sauce will keep for two weeks in the fridge.

Serve the pudding still slightly warm, cut into portions in warmed serving bowls. Ladle over the sauce and add dollops of whipped cream or ice cream.

Apple and Strawberry Crumble with Walnuts

There is nothing more delicious than a big bowl of warm crumble and this apple and strawberry one it hard to beat. I've used apple juice instead of sugar to sweeten the fruit which works brilliantly and gives an excellent result. Serve with pouring custard or vanilla ice cream - its like a hug in a bowl!

Ingredients (Serves 4)

For the Filling:
- 300ml (½ pint) apple juice
- 4 Bramley apples, peeled, cored and diced
- 6 strawberries, hulled and diced

For the Crumble:
- 100g (4oz) butter
- 175g (6oz) plain flour
- 100g (4oz) light brown sugar
- 1 tsp ground cinnamon
- 50g (2oz) shelled walnuts, finely chopped
- vanilla ice cream, to serve

Method

Preheat the oven to 190°C (375°F), Gas mark 5. To make the filling, bring the apple juice to the boil. Add the apples and bring back to just before boiling point. Remove using a slotted spoon. Place in a small bowl and stir in the strawberries and leave to cool.

To make the crumble, lightly rub the butter and flour together. Add the sugar, cinnamon and walnuts and mix together well. Spoon the cooled apples and strawberries into an ovenproof dish.

Sprinkle the crumble mixture over the fruit and bake in the oven for 30 minutes or until the top is golden brown and the fruit juices are bubbling up around the edges. Serve straight to the table and allow everyone to help themselves, adding scoops of the ice cream as you do.

Caramelised Bananas with Chocolate Mousse and Orange Caramel Sauce

This is variation on a classic 1970's dessert and its no wonder that it never seems to fade in popularity and is still going strong. Chocolate and orange are a marriage made in heaven as far as I'm concerned and the addition of the caramelised bananas gives a sensational dimension to the dish.

Ingredients (Serves 4)

- 4 bananas
- 25g (1oz) butter

For the Orange Caramel:
- 225g (8oz) caster sugar
- 1 tbsp dark rum
- 1 vanilla pod, split in half and seeds scraped out
- 150ml (¼ pint) pure orange juice

For the Chocolate Mousse
- 225g (8oz) plain chocolate, broken into squares (at least 55% cocoa solids)
- 300ml (½ pint) cream
- 3 eggs
- 1 tbsp Coole Swan or Baileys Irish Cream liqueur
- raspberries and fresh mint leaves, to decorate

Method

To make the orange caramel, place the sugar and 100ml (3½fl oz) of water in a pan and bring to the boil. Then cook until golden brown, without stirring. Stir in the rum, vanilla seeds and orange juice. This will seize but will eventually melt back together. Stir on a low heat until smooth and then remove from the heat and leave to cool.

Melt the chocolate in a heatproof bowl over a pan of simmering water. Whisk the cream in a separate bowl until soft peaks have formed. Whisk the eggs with the Coole Swan or Baileys in another heatproof bowl over a pan of simmering water until it doubles in size. It is very important to ensure the water does not boil, or it will scramble the eggs. Fold the melted chocolate into the egg mixture. Cool for 5 minutes, then using a large metal spoon, fold

in the whipped cream until well combined. Chill for two to three hours or overnight covered with clingfilm is best.

Heat an ovenproof frying pan. Cut the bananas in half. Add the butter to the heated pan and once it has stopped foaming, tip in the bananas and sauté for 2 minutes. Drizzle over a tablespoon or two of the orange caramel and cook for another 3-4 minutes until golden brown.

Arrange two pieces of banana in the centre of each serving plate. Drizzle some of the orange caramel on top and add two scoops of chocolate mousse to each one. Then drizzle the rest of the caramel orange around the mousse. Decorate with the raspberries and mint leaves to serve.

Summer Berry Pavlova

This is a recipe handed down to me by my mother, Vera. Mum is a great cook, and at one stage cooked and managed the restaurant as well as raising a family of nine. She still cooks this dessert at family get-togethers. You can enjoy this all year around, using whatever fruits are in season. Feel free to make it the day before, but don't fill until you are nearly ready to serve. A good Pavlova should have a gooey, sticky centre... almost like a marshmallow.

Ingredients (Serves 6-8)

For the Meringue:
- 4 large egg whites, at room temperature
- pinch salt
- 225g (8oz) caster sugar
- 2 tsp cornflour
- 1 tsp white wine vinegar
- 4 drops vanilla extract

For the Filling:
- 250ml (9fl oz) cream
- 1 vanilla pod, split in half and seeds scraped out
- finely grated rind of 1 orange
- 25g (1oz) icing sugar, plus a little extra for dusting
- 175g (6oz) strawberries
- 100g (4oz) raspberries
- 100g (4oz) blueberries
- 50g (2oz) blackberries
- redcurrant sprigs and fresh mint sprigs, to decorate

Method

Preheat the oven to 150°C (300°F), Gas mark 2. Line a baking sheet with parchment paper and draw on a 23cm (9in) circle. Make the meringue in a large clean bowl. Whisk the egg whites and salt into stiff peaks. Slowly add the sugar, a third at a time, whisking well between each addition until the mixture is stiffened and shiny. Sprinkle in the cornflour, vinegar and vanilla extract, then fold in gently with a metal spoon.

Pile the meringue onto the paper circle and make a deep hollow in the centre. Put in the oven and reduce heat to 120°C (240°F), Gas ½. Cook for 1½-2 hours until pale brown but a little soft in the centre. Turn off the oven, leave the door ajar and allow to cool completely.

To make the filling, whip the cream in a bowl with vanilla seeds, icing sugar and orange rind until thickened and just holding its shape. Hull the strawberries and then slice as necessary. Peel the paper off the Pavlova and transfer to a serving plate. Spread over the cream mixture and arrange the berries on top, then decorate with the redcurrant sprigs and mint sprigs and add a light dusting of icing sugar. Serve straight to the table in all its glory.

Summer Fruit Crumble with Citrus Mascarpone Cream

I just love making this in the autumn, when there are still plenty of berries around. The walnuts give great texture, but blanched hazelnuts could be used instead of the almonds if you prefer. The crumble mixture really works well on top of any fruit, and the light muscovado sugar gives the crumble its famous crunchiness. To make a large one, simply cook for 45-50 minutes, depending on the size of the dish.

Ingredients (Serves 6-8)

For the Berries:
- 100g (4oz) caster sugar
- 250ml (9fl oz) red wine
- ½ vanilla pod, split in half and seeds scraped out
- 2 whole star anise (optional)
- 1 tbsp fresh lemon juice
- 450g (1lb) mixed summer berries, such as strawberries, raspberries, blueberries and blackberries

For the Crumble:
- 75g (3oz) plain flour
- 50g (2oz) butter
- 50g (2oz) light muscovado sugar
- ½ tsp ground cinnamon
- 25g (1oz) whole blanched almonds, finely chopped
- 25g (1oz) shelled walnuts, finely chopped

For the Citrus Mascarpone Cream:
- 250g carton mascarpone cheese
- finely grated rind of 1 orange, 1 lemon and 1 lime
- ½ vanilla pod, split in half and seeds scraped out
- 1-2 tbsp sifted icing sugar

For the Caramel Sauce: (Optional)
- 125g (4 ½oz) caster sugar
- 120ml (4fl oz) cream
- 25g (1oz) butter
- fresh mint sprigs, to decorate

Method

Preheat the oven to 180°C (350°F), Gas mark 4. To prepare the berries, place the sugar in a heavy-based pan with the red wine, vanilla seeds, star anise, if using, and lemon juice. Bring to the boil, then reduce the heat and simmer for 5 minutes until slightly thickened and syrup-like. Stir in the summer berries, then remove from the heat and leave to cool.

To make the crumble, place the flour in a bowl and rub in the butter until the mixture resembles fine breadcrumbs. Stir in the sugar, cinnamon, almonds and walnuts until well combined.

Spoon the berry mixture into four individual ovenproof dishes or large ramekins. Sprinkle over the crumble mixture and arrange on a baking sheet, then bake for about 20-25 minutes until the crumble topping is golden brown and bubbling around the edges.

To make the mascarpone cream, place the mascarpone cheese in a bowl and beat in the orange, lemon and lime rind. Add the vanilla seeds and enough of the icing sugar to just sweeten, making sure it is not too sweet. Cover with clingfilm and chill in the fridge until needed. This will keep for up to three days in the fridge.

For the caramel sauce (if making), place the sugar in a heavy-based pan with 120ml (4fl oz) of water. Bring to the boil and cook for about 15 minutes or until golden brown, without stirring. If it's too dark, it will become bitter. Stir in the cream and butter and mix well to combine. Continue to cook until slightly reduced and thickened, stirring occasionally. Use immediately or leave to cool and store in the fridge. This sauce will keep for up to two weeks.

To serve, arrange the summer fruit crumbles on plates and spoon some of the citrus mascarpone cream on the side and decorate with mint sprigs, then drizzle with the caramel sauce, if using. The remainder of the caramel sauce can be served separately in a jug on the table.

Cheat's Banoffee Pie with Chocolate Drizzle

Banoffee pie always hits the spot and you can now buy jars or cans of toffee sauce in most major supermarkets which means that this dessert should take no more than 15 minutes to prepare. Ballyshiel Toffee, made by the Corrigan Gaetani family in Co. Offaly, is excellent. And if you are in a real hurry, don't bother doing the chocolate drizzle and simply crumble a Flake on top instead.

Ingredients (Serves 6)

- 250g (9oz) digestive biscuits
- 150g (5oz) butter
- rapeseed oil, for greasing
- 350g (12oz) jar toffee sauce
- 2 large ripe bananas
- 300ml (½ pint) cream
- a little caster sugar, to taste
- 25g (1oz) plain or milk chocolate, broken into squares

Method

Place the biscuits in a plastic bag and using a rolling pin, crush into fine crumbs. Melt the butter in a pan and stir in the crushed biscuits. Press the mixture into the base and up the sides of a lightly oiled, loose-bottomed fluted flan tin that is 23cm (9in) wide and 4cm (1½in) deep. Chill for 15 minutes.

Peel the bananas and thinly slice. Spread the toffee sauce over the set biscuit base and cover with the sliced bananas. Lightly whip the cream and caster sugar in a bowl until soft peaks form. Spoon on top of the bananas and spread it out to make a seal with the edge of the biscuit base. Swirl the top and chill for at least an hour.

When ready to serve, melt the chocolate in a heatproof bowl set over a pan of simmering water or use the microwave, then carefully drizzle over the cream topping. Carefully remove from the flan tin and cut into slices. Arrange on serving plates to serve.

Plum and Almond Tart

Plum and almond tart makes an ideal finish to a Sunday lunch and a friend of mine once served it with great success at their book club! I also like it with an apricot or rhubarb filling, depending on what's in season.

Ingredients (Serves 4)

- 450g (1lb) plums
- about 3 tbsp apricot jam

For the Pastry:
- 100g (4oz) butter, diced
- 175g (6oz) plain flour, plus extra for dusting
- pinch salt
- 50g (2oz) caster sugar
- 1 egg yolk
- ½ tbsp cream

For the Almond Filling:
- 100g (4oz) butter
- 100g (4oz) icing sugar
- 25g (1oz) plain flour
- 100g (4oz) ground almonds
- 2 eggs
- 1 vanilla pod, split in half and seeds scraped out
- large pinch ground cinnamon
- whipped cream and caramel ice cream, to serve

Method

To make the pastry, place the butter, flour, salt and sugar in a food mixer and blend briefly together. Add the egg yolk and cream and mix until the pastry just comes together. Do not over-work or the pastry will be tough. Cover in clingfilm, then chill for one hour.

To make the filling, cream the butter and sugar together in a large bowl until pale in colour. Gradually add in the flour and almonds, then beat in the eggs, vanilla seeds and cinnamon. Beat for 5 minutes until light and fluffy.

Meanwhile, preheat oven to 190°C (375°F), Gas mark 5. Roll out the pastry on a lightly floured board and use to line a 23cm (9in) loose-bottomed flan tin. Chill again for 15 minutes.

Meanwhile, cut the plums into wedges, discarding the stones. Spread the almond filling into the pastry case. Arrange the plum wedges on top in a fan shape and gently press the plums down into the filling. Bake for 25-30 minutes or until the almond filling is cooked through and the tart is golden brown on top.

Just before the tart comes out of the oven, warm the apricot jam in a small pan and then use to brush all over the top of the tart. Remove the tart from the tin and transfer to a plate. Cut into slices and arrange on warmed serving plates. Serve at once with the whipped cream and caramel ice cream.

Chocolate Coffee Roulade

This delightful, rich chocolate coffee roulade always goes down a treat, and even if you are watching the calories a little goes a long way... It has the added bonus that it is really quick to make and you can prepare it ahead, leaving you with very little to do at the last minute.

Ingredients (Serves 6-8)

- a little butter, for greasing
- 100g (4oz) plain chocolate, broken into squares (at least 55% cocoa solids)
- 4 eggs, separated
- 100g (4oz) caster sugar
- 1 tbsp Tia Maria liqueur (optional)
- 2 tbsp strong black coffee
- 300ml (½ pint) cream
- 100g (4oz) toasted shelled walnuts, finely chopped
- icing sugar, to dust

Method

Preheat the oven to 180°C (350°F), Gas mark 4. Lightly butter a 33 x 23cm (13 x 9in) Swiss roll tin and line with parchment paper.

Place the chocolate in a heatproof bowl set over a pan of simmering water and leave to melt. Remove from the heat and leave to cool a little. Whisk the egg yolks and sugar together in a large bowl for about 4 minutes until very pale.

Whisk the egg whites in a separate bowl until stiff. Using a large metal spoon, fold in the melted chocolate. Finally fold in the egg whites until just combined.

Pour the chocolate mixture into the prepared tin and use a palette knife to spread it out evenly. Bake for about 12 minutes until well risen and firm to the touch.

Turn the sponge out onto a sheet of parchment paper generously sprinkled with icing sugar. Carefully peel off the lining paper. Cover the roulade with a warm, damp tea towel and leave to cool.

To make the filling, place the cream in a bowl and gently whisk with an electric mixer until stiff. Then fold in the Tia Maria, if using and the coffee, then spread the flavoured cream over the cold roulade. Sprinkle the walnuts on top. Using the parchment to help, roll up the roulade to enclose the filling.

To serve, transfer the roulade on to a serving plate and dust with icing sugar, then cut into slices and arrange on serving plates.

Terrine of Vanilla Ice Cream with Meringue & Blackberry Sauce

This terrine is really more like a frozen parfait. It can be made without a special ice cream machine. It is perfect if you have large numbers to feed and really must be made a day before you want to serve it.

Ingredients (Serves 10-12)

For the Meringue:
- 2 egg whites, at room temperature
- 50g (2oz) caster sugar
- 50g (2oz) icing sugar, sifted

For the Ice Cream:
- 2 gelatine leaves
- 1 litre (1 ¾ pints) milk
- 100g (4oz) granulated sugar
- 1 vanilla pod, split in half and seeds scraped out
- 12 egg yolks
- 60g (2½oz) caster sugar

For the Blackberry Sauce:
- 450g (1lb) blackberries
- 250g (9oz) sugar

Method

First, make the meringues. Preheat the oven to 120°C (240°F), Gas mark ½. Whisk the egg whites in a bowl until stiff, then slowly add the caster sugar, whisking until completely dissolved. Finally gently fold in the icing sugar. Fill a piping bag fitted with a star shaped nozzle and pipe the meringue mixture into four small circular shapes on a parchment lined baking sheet. Bake for about 1½ hours to dry out without colouring. Leave to cool completely and then store in an airtight container until needed.

Next make the ice cream. Place the gelatine in a bowl and cover with cold water, then set aside for 10 minutes until softened. Heat the milk with the granulated sugar and split the vanilla pod. When just boiling, remove from the heat, then cover and leave for 10 minutes to infuse.

Meanwhile, beat the egg yolks with the caster sugar and vanilla seeds until the sugar has completely dissolved and the mixture is creamy. Bring the milk infusion back to the boil, then add to the yolk mixture, whisking constantly. Return to the rinsed pan and cook over a medium heat, whisking all the time, until the mixture coats the back of a spoon. Be very careful not to overcook. Then strain through a very fine sieve into a clean bowl.

Drain the gelatine and squeeze out the excess water. Then whisk the softened gelatine into the milk mixture and allow to cool, whisking occasionally. When cold, churn the mixture in an ice cream maker until thickened or place in the freezer and keep whisking every 20 minutes until almost frozen.

To make the blackberry sauce, place the blackberries in a pan with the sugar and bring to the boil. Reduce the heat and stir gently for a few minutes until the sugar has dissolved and the blackberries have softened. Remove from the heat and leave to cool.

To assemble the terrine, line a 1.75 litre (3 pint) loaf tin with overlapping clingfilm. Break up the meringues and use to fill the bottom of the lined tin. Add half of the ice cream, using a palette knife to get it into the corners and then cover with half of the poached blackberries. Cover with the rest of the ice cream and then bring up the clingfilm to enclose completely. Place in the freezer in a rigid plastic container for at least six hours or overnight is best.

Place the rest of the poached blackberries in a liquidiser and blend to a purée, adding a little water if it seems too thick. Pass through a fine sieve into a jug and cover with clingfilm. Chill until needed.

When ready to serve, briefly dip the loaf tin in boiling water and then turn out on to serving platter. Using a sharp knife dipped with boiling water, cut into slices and arrange on serving plates with the blackberry sauce to serve.

Baking

Brown Scones

Brown scones are full of roughage and great for breakfast. And here is a good tip: you can make this mixture, shape the scones and freeze them. You can then cook the scones straight from freezer to oven. Give them about an extra 5 minutes. Simply check the scones are golden brown and well risen just as if cooking straight away.

Ingredients
(Makes about 20)

- rapeseed oil, for greasing
- 450g (1lb) plain flour, plus extra for dusting
- 450g (1lb) coarse wholemeal flour
- 1 tsp baking soda
- 1 tsp salt
- 50g (2oz) butter
- 1 tbsp light brown sugar
- 100g (4oz) wheat bran
- 1 tbsp golden syrup
- 600ml (1 pint) buttermilk, plus a little extra if necessary
- butter or lightly whipped cream and strawberry jam, to serve

Method

Preheat the oven to 220°C (425°F), Gas mark 7. Sift the flours, baking soda and salt into a bowl. Tip in the bran left in the sieve and stir in with the wheat bran. Rub in the butter with your fingertips until evenly dispersed. Stir the sugar and wheat bran through.

Make a well in the centre of the dry ingredients and add the golden syrup and buttermilk. Using a large spoon, mix gently and quickly until you have achieved a smooth, not-too-sticky dough. Add a little bit more buttermilk, if necessary, until the dough binds together without being sloppy.

On a lightly floured surface, lightly roll out the dough to a 2cm (¾in) thickness and cut into rounds with a 6cm (2½in) plain cutter. Arrange on a couple of large baking sheets lined with greased parchment paper and bake for 10-15 minutes, until golden brown and well risen. Serve on serving plates with cream or butter and strawberry jam.

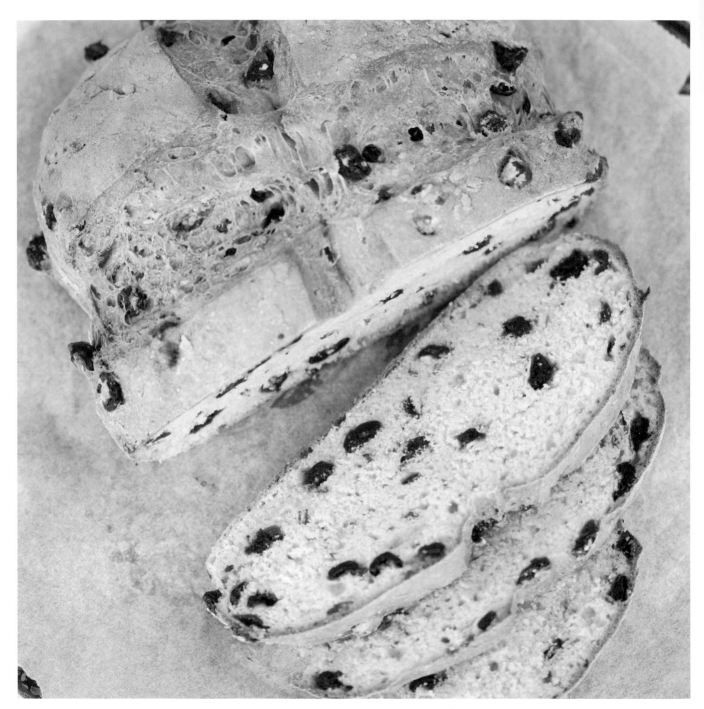

Cranberry and Rosemary Bread

I have a wonderful breakfast chef working with me in the restaurant. Her name is Marie McGloine and every morning she makes this cranberry and rosemary bread for our overnight guests. She is the best baker I have ever seen. We bake yeast breads too but this is a traditional Irish soda bread with a twist.

Ingredients
(Makes one loaf)

- 450g (1lb) plain flour, plus extra for dusting
- 1 tsp bicarbonate of soda
- 1 tsp salt
- 100g (4oz) dried cranberries
- 4 fresh rosemary sprigs, leaves stripped and finely chopped
- 350ml (12fl oz) buttermilk, plus a little extra if necessary
- butter, to serve

Method

Preheat the oven to 220°C (425°F), Gas mark 7. Sift the flour, bicarbonate of soda and salt into a bowl. Stir the cranberries and rosemary through and make a well in the centre. Then add the buttermilk and, using a large spoon, mix gently and quickly until you have achieved a nice soft dough. Add a little bit more buttermilk if necessary until the dough binds together without being sloppy.

Knead the dough very lightly on a lightly floured surface and then shape into a round that is roughly 15cm (6in) in size. Place on a non-stick baking sheet and cut a deep cross in the top.

Bake for 15 minutes, then reduce the temperature to 200°C (400°F), Gas mark 6 and bake for another 20-25 minutes or until the loaf is evenly golden and crusty. To check that this loaf is properly cooked, tap the base. It should sound hollow. If it doesn't, return it to the oven for another 5 minutes.

Transfer the cooked soda bread to a wire rack and leave to cool for about 20 minutes. This bread is best eaten while it is still warm. To serve, place the soda bread on a breadboard and cut into slices at the table. Have a dish of butter on hand for spreading.

Brown Wheaten Bread

This is the first thing we make every morning at the restaurant so that guests who have stayed overnight wake up to the smell of baking bread wafting around the house. It is delicious sprinkled with a couple of tablespoons of sesame or sunflower seeds or porridge oats before baking. If you don't have any buttermilk in the house sour ordinary milk with the juice of a lemon will suffice. Our breakfasts are served each morning by Imelda Oats and I always know she will be in to the kitchen so I can come and chat to people who want this brown bread recipe. Add your own butter and marmalade to taste!

Ingredients (Makes 3 x 900ml (1½ pint) Loaves)

- rapeseed oil, for greasing
- 450g (1lb) plain flour, plus extra for dusting
- 450g (1lb) coarse wholemeal flour
- 1 tsp baking soda
- 1 tsp salt
- 100g (4oz) wheat bran
- 50g (2oz) butter
- 1 tbsp golden syrup
- 1 tbsp light brown sugar
- 600ml (1 pint) buttermilk, plus a little extra if necessary
- butter for spreading, to serve

Method

Preheat the oven to 180°C (350°F), Gas mark 4 and lightly oil 3 x 900ml (1½ pint) loaf tins. Sift the plain flour, baking soda and salt into a bowl. Tip in the bran left in the sieve, and stir in with the wholemeal flour and wheat bran.

Rub in the butter with your fingertips until evenly dispersed. Make a well in the centre of the dry ingredients and add the golden syrup, brown sugar and buttermilk. Using a large spoon, mix gently and quickly until you have achieved a nice dropping consistency. Add a little bit more buttermilk if necessary, until the dough binds together without being sloppy.

Divide the dough into three equal pieces and place in the prepared loaf tins. Bake for 25 minutes and then check that the loaves are not browning too much. If they are, reduce the temperature or move the loaves down in the oven, then bake for a further 20 minutes until cooked through and each one has a slightly cracked top.

To check the loaves are properly cooked, tip each one out of the tin and tap the base. It should sound hollow. If it doesn't, return it to the oven for another 5 minutes. Tip out on to a wire rack and leave to cool completely. To serve, place the brown wheaten bread on a bread board and cut into slices at the table. Hand around with a separate pot of butter for spreading.

Madeira Cake

Madeira cake is a great afternoon treat. Try it with a dash of rum and you might also like to add a little rind from an orange or lemon or a mixture of both. Alternatively, some chopped nuts would work well. Remember to keep any leftovers for a trifle.

Ingredients (Serves 8)

- 200g (7oz) self-raising flour
- 175g (6oz) unsalted butter
- 175g (6oz) caster sugar
- 3 eggs
- 25g (1oz) ground almonds or fine polenta
- finely grated rind of 1 lemon
- 1 tsp vanilla extract
- 1 tbsp milk

Method

Preheat the oven to 180°C (350°F), Gas Mark 4. Sift the flour into a bowl and set aside until needed. Cut the butter into small cubes into the bowl of a mixer fitted with a paddle attachment. Add the sugar. Beat until it turns into a pale cream.

With the motor running, add one egg with a tablespoon of the sifted flour to stop the egg curdling, then add the other two eggs. When the eggs are incorporated, add the almonds or polenta with the lemon rind and whizz again.

Take the lid off the processor and add the rest of the sifted flour with the vanilla extract and milk. Whizz again until you have a smooth cake mixture, scraping the sides of the bowl with a spatula if you need to.

Pour the cake mixture into a 900g (2lb) non-stick loaf tin, levelling off the top. Bake in the lower middle shelf of the oven, checking it after 45 minutes. Check and see if a skewer comes out clean. If not, cook it for another 5-10 minutes until it is cooked through. This will depend on your oven and the size of the tin you use. Leave to cool in the tin for 10 minutes, before turning it out on to a wire rack to cool completely.

To serve, cut into slices and arrange on a serving plate.

Coeliac Christmas Pudding

This gluten-free recipe for Christmas pudding is so tasty that non-coeliacs will love it too. It is much lighter than traditional Christmas pudding; however, it does not keep as long, so store it in a cool, dry container for about three weeks, maximum. This pudding should serve 8-10 people as a rough guide but realistically, it goes much further.

Ingredients
(Makes one 1.2-1.4 Litre (2-2½ Pint) Pudding)

- 150g (5oz) fresh gluten-free bread
- 100g (4oz) butter, plus a little extra for greasing
- 50g (2oz) rice flour
- ½ tsp ground cinnamon
- 1 tsp mixed spice
- ½ tsp gluten-free baking powder
- 100g (4oz) Bramley apples, cored, peeled and grated
- 100g (4oz) carrot, grated
- 400g (14oz) mixed dried fruit
- 100g (4oz) light muscovado sugar
- 50g (2oz) chopped mixed peel
- 50g (2oz) ground almonds
- 1 tbsp black treacle
- 2 eggs, beaten
- finely grated rind of ½ lemon and ½ orange
- 2 tbsp dark rum
- pouring custard or brandy butter, to serve

Method

Break the bread into pieces and whizz to fine crumbs in a food processor. Set aside.

Grease and line the base of a 1.2-1.4 litre (2- 2½ pint) pudding basin with parchment paper. Sift together the rice flour, spices and baking powder.

Melt the butter in a small pan or in the microwave, then leave to cool a little. Add to the flour mixture with the apples, carrot, dried fruit, breadcrumbs, sugar, peel and ground almonds. Mix thoroughly to combine.

Heat the treacle in a small pan or dish in the microwave until just warm. Remove from the heat. Add in the eggs, citrus rind and rum. Mix into the flour and fruit. Then spoon the mixture into the prepared pudding basin. Cover with a double thickness of parchment paper. Tie to secure and over wrap in foil.

To cook the pudding, stand in a large cake tin and fill three-quarters full of boiling water. Cover the tin with foil. Steam for four hours until the pudding has risen and is firm to the touch, topping up the water as necessary.

Leave the Christmas pudding to cool completely, then cover the top of the pudding with parchment paper and wrap in foil. Store in a cool, dry place. To reheat, steam for two hours and then turn out on to a serving plate. Cut into portions and place in wide-rimmed warmed serving bowls. Add a little pouring custard or brandy butter to serve.

Tunisian Orange Cake

When you feel the evenings drawing in, this is the cake to bake. It is a great time of year to bake with the kitchen door open and the wonderful smells wafting around. I love to cook something tasty and sweet these evenings, as we enjoy the last of the summer sunsets. A little of what you fancy does you good and this moist orange cake is a favourite in our house.

Ingredients (Serves 6-8)

- a little butter, for greasing
- a little plain flour, for dusting
- 50g (2oz) slightly stale white breadcrumbs
- 100g (4oz) caster sugar
- 100g (4oz) ground almonds
- 1 ½ tsp baking powder
- 200ml (7fl oz) sunflower oil
- 4 eggs
- finely grated rind of 1 large orange (preferably unwaxed)
- finely grated rind of ½ lemon (preferably unwaxed)

For the Citrus Syrup:
- juice of 1 orange (preferably unwaxed)
- juice of ½ lemon (preferably unwaxed)
- 75g (3oz) sugar
- 2 whole cloves
- 1 cinnamon stick
- lightly whipped cream or Greek yoghurt or crème fraîche, to serve

Method

Line the base of a 20cm (8in) round cake tin that is at least 5cm (2in) with parchment paper. Then grease and flour the tin, shaking out any excess.

Mix the breadcrumbs in a large bowl with the sugar, ground almonds and baking powder. Whisk the oil in a jug with the eggs. Pour into the breadcrumb mixture and mix well to combine.

Stir the orange and lemon rind into the cake mixture and then with the aid of a white spatula, transfer to the prepared tin. Put in a cold oven and turn on with the heat set to 180°C (350°F), Gas mark 4 and bake for 45-60 minutes or until the cake is cooked through and golden brown. A skewer inserted into the centre should come out clean. Allow to cool for 5 minutes before turning out onto a serving plate.

Meanwhile, make the citrus syrup. Put the lemon and orange juice into a pan with the sugar, cloves and cinnamon stick. Bring gently to the boil, stirring until the sugar has dissolved completely. Reduce the heat and simmer for another 3 minutes until slightly reduced.

While the cake is still warm, pierce it with a skewer. Spoon the hot syrup all over the cake. Leave to cool. Spoon the excess syrup back over the cake every now and then until it is all completely soaked up. You can remove the cloves and cinnamon stick if you want to, but leave them on top of the cake as they look very attractive and will continue to add flavour.

Cut the cake into slices and arrange on serving plates with a dollop of lightly whipped cream, Greek yoghurt or crème fraîche.

Gluten-Free Chocolate Tart

This is a wonderful chocolate tart that is suitable for coeliacs. It uses a number of different types of flour, none of which contain any gluten to create a really lovely texture. Look out for xanthan gum in the specialist heath food section of larger supermarkets or you will also find it in health food stores. It is a thickener that is often used in gluten-free baking and helps to provide the 'stickiness' that is normally provided by gluten.

Ingredients (Serves 8-10)

For the Pastry:
- 100g (4oz) rice flour
- 100g (4oz) polenta (fine cornmeal)
- 100g (4oz) potato flour, plus a little extra for dusting
- 2 tsp xanthan gum
- 225g (8oz) butter
- 50g (2oz) caster sugar
- 2 eggs

For the Filling:
- (450g) (1lb) plain chocolate (minimum 55% cocoa solids)
- 1 tsp cocoa powder
- 4 eggs
- 75g (3oz) caster sugar
- 300ml (½ pint) cream
- 150ml (¼ pint) milk
- lightly whipped cream, to serve

Method

To make the pastry, place the rice flour, polenta, potato flour, xanthan gum, butter, sugar and eggs in a food processor. Blend together briefly until a pastry dough has just formed. Do not over-work or the pastry will become very tough. Gather the dough up and gently shape into a ball. Wrap in clingfilm and chill for one hour.

Roll out the pastry on a lightly floured work surface and use to line a 23cm (9in) loose-bottomed flan tin. Brush off any excess potato flour with a pastry brush and then chill for another 30 minutes. Bake blind for about 20 minutes or until the pastry is cooked through and lightly golden.

Reduce the oven temperature to 100°C (200°F), Gas mark ¼ and make the filling. Place the chocolate, cocoa powder, eggs and sugar in a large bowl. Boil the cream and milk together in a small pan. Pour the hot milk and cream mix over chocolate mixture and whisk until smooth, then pass through a fine sieve into a jug.

Pour the chocolate filling into the prepared pastry case and bake for 30-40 minutes or until the filling is just cooked through but still had a slight wobble in the centre. If you have remaining mixture, this will keep for up to a week in the fridge.

Leave the tart to cool at room temperature and then carefully remove from the tin and place on a plate. Cut into slices and arrange on serving plates with dollops of the cream to serve.

Rhubarb and Ginger Crumble Cake

This rhubarb and ginger crumble cake is best served warm as a pudding or cold as a teatime treat. I like it with whipped cream, but it would also be good with crème fraîche, clotted cream, vanilla ice cream or custard – the list is endless! If you don't fancy the rhubarb, try using apples, plums or blackberries, depending on the time of year.

Ingredients (Serves 6-8)

For the Crumble:
- 125g (4½oz) plain flour
- 4 tbsp caster sugar
- 75g (3oz) butter, at room temperature
- pinch ground cinnamon

For the Fruit:
- 750 g (1¾ lb) rhubarb, trimmed and cut into 1cm (½in) pieces
- 1 tbsp caster sugar
- 1 tsp ground ginger

For the Cake:
- 175g (6oz) butter, at room temperature, plus extra for greasing
- 175g (6oz) caster sugar
- 3 eggs, beaten
- 175g (6oz) plain flour
- 2 tsp baking powder
- 1 tbsp milk
- whipped cream, to serve

Method

Heat the oven to 190°C (375°F), Gas mark 5. Butter a 23cm (9in) loose-bottomed cake tin, line the base with parchment paper. To make the crumble topping, place the flour, sugar, butter and cinnamon in a food processor, then pulse until crumbly. To prepare the fruit, place the rhubarb in a bowl and tip in the sugar and ginger. Toss until evenly coated. Set both aside.

To make the cake, beat the butter and sugar together in a bowl until light and fluffy. Beat in the eggs, a little at a time, adding one tablespoon of the flour when you have added about half of the beaten eggs. This will stop it from curdling. Sift over the rest of the flour and the baking powder, then fold gently but thoroughly. Finally, fold in the milk.

Spread the cake mixture over the base of the prepared cake tin, pile the sugared rhubarb on top, then sprinkle over the crumble topping.

Bake for about one hour until the sides of the cake have shrunk slightly away from the tin, the rhubarb is soft and the crumble is golden brown. To test if the cake is done, insert a fine metal skewer into the middle. If it comes out clean, the cake is ready.

Remove the cake from the oven and leave to cool in the tin for 15 minutes set on a wire rack. To serve, cut the rhubarb and ginger crumble cake into slices and arrange on serving plates with dollops of whipped cream.

Mango and Maple Cake

Of course, you could use apricots, peaches or even pineapple instead of the mango, if you prefer and depending on the time of year you are making it. We buy all our vanilla on line from a website called www.vanillabazaar.com. They stock a wide range of products so it's well worth checking them out.

Ingredients (Serves 8)

- 125g (4 ½oz) butter
- 150g (5oz) light muscovado sugar
- 100g (4oz) maple syrup
- 150g (5oz) plain flour
- 100g (4oz) wholemeal flour
- 2 tsp baking powder
- 1 tsp ground cinnamon
- 2 ripe mangoes, peeled, stoned and finely chopped
- 100g (4oz) pecan nuts, roughly chopped

For the Topping:
- finely grated rind and juice of 1 orange
- 200g (7oz) soft cream cheese
- 50g (2oz) icing sugar
- ½ vanilla pod, split in half and seeds scraped out

Method

Preheat oven to 160°C (325°F), Gas mark 3. Place the butter, sugar and maple syrup in a small pan and heat gently until melted, stirring occasionally.

Sift together the plain and wholemeal flour into a large bowl with the baking powder and cinnamon, then tip in any remaining wheat flakes left in the sieve. Stir in the melted syrup mixture, then fold in the mangoes and pecan nuts.

Spoon the mixture into a non-stick 900g (2lb) loaf tin and bake for 1½ hours until well risen and golden brown. To test if the cake is done, stick a fine metal skewer into the centre of the cake; it should come out clean. Leave the cake to cool in the tin for 5 minutes, then turn out onto a wire rack and leave to cool completely.

Optional: To make the topping, mix the orange rind in a bowl with the soft cream cheese, icing sugar and vanilla seeds, then stir in enough of the orange juice to make smooth icing. Spread thickly over the top of the cooked cake. To serve, cut the mango and maple cake into slices and place on serving plates.

Simnel Cake

Simnel cake is the traditional Easter cake. You can make it a few days ahead and enjoy it again on Easter Monday with a cup of tea. The marzipan balls on top of the cake represent 11 of the apostles, not surprisingly Judas isn't included!

Ingredients (Serves 10-12)

- 225g (8oz) plain flour
- 500g (18oz) dried fruits, such as sultanas, raisins, currants, mixed peel, ready-to-eat apricots or prunes
- finely grated rind and juice of 1 lemon
- 175g (6oz) butter, softened, plus extra for greasing
- 175g (6oz) light muscovado sugar
- 4 eggs, beaten
- 1 tsp ground cinnamon
- ½ tsp freshly grated nutmeg
- 100g (4oz) toasted flaked almonds
- 2 x 250g packets golden marzipan
- 1 egg white, lightly beaten

Method

Preheat the oven to 160°C (325°F), Gas mark 3. Line the base and sides of a 20cm (8in) loose-bottomed cake tin with parchment paper. Sift the flour into a bowl and set aside until needed.

Depending on what selection of dried fruit you have decided to use, you may need to chop some of them up so that everything is equal in size. Toss all of the dried fruit in a bowl with the lemon rind and juice and set aside.

Cream the butter and sugar together in a food mixer (or with a hand held whisk) until pale and creamy. Add the eggs bit by bit with a little of the flour each time also, beating after each addition. Add the remaining flour with the cinnamon and nutmeg and fold through to combine. Add the dried fruits and lemon mixture with the flaked almonds, stirring well to combine.

Finally, cut half of the marzipan into small cubes and gently fold into the cake mixture. Using a spatula, transfer to the prepared tin and smooth down the top. Bake for about two hours or until a skewer comes out clean when inserted into the centre. Leave to cool in the tin, then carefully remove and place on a flat plate.

Once the cake has completely cooled, preheat the grill to high. Roll out the remaining marzipan to about 5mm (¼in) thick and cut out a 20cm (8in) round using the clean base of the cake tin as a guide. Brush the top of the cake with the egg white and lay the circle of marzipan on to stick. Use the point of a finger to push the marzipan into a wavy effect around the edge, then brush all over the top with the egg white.

Roll the marzipan trimmings into 11 equal-size balls and arrange them on top in an even circle about 2.5cm (1in) in from the edge. Brush the balls with egg white also, then grill the cake for a few minutes until turning golden brown in places. Place the cake on a serving plate or cake stand and decorate with ribbons around the edge. Serve straight to the table.

Warm Chocolate Brownie with Fudge Sauce

There is definitely something about chocolate that is addictive. It contains several stimulants, including caffeine and pleasure-inducing endorphins. These are intensely chocolaty brownies, which get smothered in a rich fudge sauce that is flavoured with – you've guessed it – more chocolate! If the brownies have gone cold and you want to heat them up in a hurry, pour over some of the fudge sauce and flash under a hot grill until bubbling.

Ingredients (Serves 8-10)

For the Brownie:
- 400g plain chocolate, finely chopped (at least 55% cocoa solids)
- 225g (8oz) butter
- 4 eggs
- 275g (10oz) caster sugar
- 100g (4oz) self-raising flour
- 75g (3oz) cocoa powder
- 100g (4oz) mixed nuts, roughly chopped

For the Fudge Sauce:
- 150ml (¼ pint) cream
- 50g (2oz) caster sugar
- 25g (1oz) butter
- 175g (6oz) plain chocolate, finely chopped (at least 55% cocoa solids)
- vanilla ice cream, to serve

Method

Preheat the oven to 160°C (325°F), Gas mark 3. Place 100g (4oz) of the chocolate in a heatproof bowl with the butter and set over a pan of simmering water until melted; then stir to combine. Remove from the heat and leave to cool a little.

Meanwhile, whisk the eggs in a bowl until stiff and holding their shape, then whisk in the sugar until you have achieved a stiff sabayon that can hold a trail of the figure eight. Sift the flour and cocoa powder into the sabayon and lightly fold in. Add the melted chocolate mixture with the remaining finely chopped chocolate and the nuts, and continue folding gently until all the ingredients are just combined.

Pour the chocolate mixture into a deep-sided baking tin that is about 27.5 x 18cm (11 x 7in), lined with parchment paper. Bake for 35-40 minutes until the top is crusty but the centre is still a little soft. Meanwhile, make the fudge sauce. Place the cream in a pan with the sugar and butter and bring to the boil, stirring. Reduce the heat and simmer gently for a few minutes, until thickened and toffee-like, stirring occasionally to prevent the mixture from catching. Remove from heat and leave to cool.

Place the chocolate for the sauce in a heatproof bowl set over a pan of simmering water until melted. Whisk into the cream until smooth and well combined. Leave to cool completely, then transfer to a bowl. Cover with clingfilm and keep in the fridge until needed. It should keep happily for up to one week.

Remove brownies from the oven and allow to cool in the tin for about 5 minutes, then remove from the tin and peel off the parchment paper. Transfer the fudge sauce to a pan and gently heat through, or pierce the clingfilm and heat in the microwave. Cut the brownies into rectangles and arrange on serving plates with the hot fudge sauce and scoops of ice cream.

Chocolate Cup Cakes

These delicious cup cakes take no time at all to make and will be a guaranteed hit with all of the family. They are also perfect to take on picnics or in lunch boxes (as long as the school allows the odd treat!). Simply wrap gently in greaseproof paper or put in rigid plastic containers to transport. Don't worry if your tin is not non stick simply line with deep paper cases.

Ingredients (Serves 12)

- 250g (9oz) butter, at room temperature, plus extra for greasing
- 175g (6oz) self-raising flour, sifted
- 250g (9oz) caster sugar
- 4 eggs
- 1 tsp vanilla extract
- 25g (1oz) plain flour, sifted
- 25g (1oz) cocoa powder, sifted
- 175ml (6fl oz) milk
- 24 mini Easter eggs

For the Chocolate Icing:
- 225g (8oz) icing sugar, sifted
- 2 tbsp chocolate and hazelnut spread (from Wicklow fine food company)
- 100g (4oz) plain chocolate, broken into squares (at least 55% cocoa solids)

Method

Preheat oven to 180°C (350°F), Gas mark 4. Grease a 12-hole non-stick muffin tin. Place the butter and sugar in a bowl and beat until pale and creamy. Add a little of the flour, then slowly add eggs and vanilla extract, mixing well to combine.

Slowly add the remaining flour and cocoa powder to the butter and sugar mixture with the milk and beat until just smooth. Divide the mixture between the muffin holes and bake for 20 minutes until well risen and golden brown. Remove from the oven and leave to sit for 10 minutes in the tin. Turn the cup cakes out on to a wire rack to cool completely.

Meanwhile, make the icing. Mix the icing sugar in a bowl with one tablespoon of water to make a thick paste. Melt the chocolate in the microwave in a heatproof bowl or set over a pan of simmering water. Leave to cool a little, then stir in the icing sugar paste and add the chocolate and hazelnut spread, beating with a wooden spoon until smooth.

Cover the cooled cup cakes with the chocolate icing. The mixture will harden quite quickly, so use a small palette knife dipped in boiling water to help spread it evenly on top of the cupcakes. Top each one with mini eggs and wrap with colourful ribbons or florist's sisal (which you can buy from any good florist) to create a nest effect. Arrange on a serving plate in a pyramid to serve.

Apricot and Almond Cake with Oranges and Caramel

For a Sunday treat or a dinner party at any time of the year – you will not go far wrong with this apricot and almond cake with oranges and caramel. This caramel sauce is delicious and really easy to make

Ingredients (Serves 6-8)

- 225g (8oz) butter
- 225g (8oz) caster sugar
- juice of 1 lemon
- 75g (3oz) ground almonds
- 100g (4oz) plain flour
- 100g (4oz) dried apricots, chopped in the food processor
- 3 large eggs, beaten

Oranges in Caramel:
- 4 large oranges, peeled and cut into segments
- 4 tbsp sugar

Method

Preheat the oven to 180°C (350°F), Gas Mark 4. Line a shallow 23cm (9in) loose-bottomed cake tin with parchment paper. Beat the butter and sugar together in a bowl until light and fluffy, then mix in the lemon juice and ground almonds. Fold in the flour, apricots and eggs. Transfer the mixture to the lined cake tin, smooth the top with a palette knife and bake for about 35 minutes or until golden brown and firm to the touch. Leave to settle in the tin for 5 minutes then transfer to a wire rack and leave to cool completely.

Optional: To make the oranges in caramel, place the oranges in a flat dish. Heat the sugar in a heavy-based pan, allowing it to brown, then add 150ml (¼ pint) of water and boil until you have a caramel sauce. Pour it over the oranges and leave to cool completely. Transfer the apricot and almond cake to a plate, then cut into slices and arrange on serving plates. Spoon over the oranges in caramel to serve.

Homemade Apple Tart

It is hard to beat this homemade apple tart and whenever I make one, it's smell transports me back to my childhood. Feel free to mix the apples with blackberries or try a mixture of rhubarb and strawberry, depending on what is in season. To make your tart extra special, add a vanilla pod to your bag of sugar and leave for at least a week before using.

Ingredients (Serves 6-8)

- 225g (8oz) plain flour, plus extra for dusting
- 2 tbsp icing sugar
- 100g (4oz) butter
- 2 large egg yolks
- 900g (2lb) Bramley cooking apples
- 100g (4oz) golden caster sugar
- 1/4 tsp ground cinnamon
- good pinch ground cloves
- 1 tbsp milk

Method

Sift the flour and icing sugar into a bowl. Using a round-bladed knife, work in the butter and then mix in the egg yolks with two to three tablespoons of ice-cold water until the dough just comes together. Wrap in clingfilm and chill for at least 30 minutes.

Preheat the oven to 190°C (375°F), Gas mark 5. Lightly dust the work surface with flour. Divide the pastry into two portions, one slightly larger than the other, then roll out the larger piece until it's about 30cm (12in) in diameter. Use to line a 20cm (8in) pie dish or 23cm (9in) flat plate, gently pressing into the corners. Knock the sides with a round-bladed knife to give a decorative finish and place back in the fridge to chill while you prepare the apples.

Peel, core and slice the apples. Place in a large bowl with all but one tablespoon of the caster sugar and the cinnamon and cloves. Brush the edge of the pastry with a little milk. Mix together, then pile into the lined pie dish. Roll out the second piece of pastry into a circle slightly larger than the pie dish and use to cover the apples. Press the edges together to seal, then use a sharp knife to cut away any excess.

Crimp the edges of the tart with a round-bladed knife and using your fingers as a guide, roll out the pastry scraps and cut into leaf shapes. Brush with milk and stick on top of the pie. Brush with milk and sprinkle with the rest of the sugar. Bake for 25-30 minutes, then reduce the oven to 180°C (350°F), Gas mark 4 and bake for 20-25 minutes until golden brown. Cut into slices and put on plates to serve.

Essentials

Tomato Sauce

If tomatoes are not in season it is much better to use a can of chopped tomatoes otherwise you could end with a very tasteless mush! If using fresh tomatoes, you'll need to remove their skins. Simply cut a light cross on the bottom of each tomato, using a sharp knife. Pop them into a bowl of boiling water for about 45 seconds, then peel off the skins. This will keep happily in the fridge for up to one week covered with clingfilm. I often add a little shredded fresh basil just before serving for a more pronounced flavour.

Ingredients
(Makes about 350ml (12fl oz))

- 1 tbsp rapeseed oil
- 1 onion, finely chopped
- 1 garlic clove, crushed
- 6 large ripe tomatoes, peeled, seeded and cut into chunks or 400g can chopped tomatoes
- 2 tsp red wine vinegar
- 1 tsp caster sugar
- 2 tsp tomato purée
- Maldon sea salt and freshly ground black pepper

Method

Heat the oil in a pan and sauté the onion and garlic for a few minutes until softened but not coloured. Tip in the tomatoes with the vinegar, sugar and tomato purée. Cook on a low heat for a few minutes while stirring to help break the tomatoes down Season to taste. Then simmer gently for about 25-30 minutes until the sauce has reduced and dried out a little. Use immediately or leave to cool, transfer to a bowl and cover with clingfilm, then chill until needed.

Basil Pesto

This will keep happily in the fridge for up to one week just keep topped up with a little extra rapeseed oil to keep it tasting lovely and fresh. It's great just stirred into pasta for an instant supper. To make walnut pesto simply replace the toasted pine kernels with toasted shelled walnuts. This version is also great when made with flat-leaf parsley instead of the basil and pecorino instead of the Parmesan.

Ingredients
(Makes about 250ml (9fl oz))

- 1 large bunch of fresh basil leaves (at least 50g (2oz))
- 2 garlic cloves, peeled
- 25g (1oz) toasted pine kernels
- 175ml (6fl oz) rapeseed oil
- 50g (2oz) freshly grated Parmesan
- Maldon sea salt and freshly ground black pepper

Method

Place the basil in a food processor with the garlic, pine nuts and a quarter of the oil. Blend to a paste, then slowly add the remaining oil through the feeder tube. Transfer to a bowl and fold in the Parmesan, then season to taste. Cover with clingfilm and chill until needed.

Béchamel Sauce

This classic white sauce is necessary for so many dishes in the kitchen and is actually extremely easy to make. I've never understood why you can buy packets of it that you just need to add liquid to in the supermarket! Depending on how you intend on using it, it can be flavoured with some chopped fresh flat-leaf parsley or chives, a dollop of your favourite mustard or a handful of grated cheese. You can also replace some of the milk with stock for a lighter result.

Ingredients
(Makes about 300ml (½ Pint))

- 450ml (¾ pint) milk
- 1 small onion, roughly chopped
- 1 bay leaf
- ½ tsp black peppercorns
- 25g (1oz) butter
- 25g (1oz) plain flour
- pinch freshly grated nutmeg
- Maldon sea salt and freshly ground white pepper

Method

Place the milk in a pan with the onion, bay leaf and peppercorns. Bring to scalding point, then remove from the heat, cover and set aside to infuse for at least 10 and up to 30 minutes Strain through a sieve into a jug.

Wipe out the pan and use to melt the butter. Stir in the flour and cook for 1 minute, stirring. Remove from the heat and gradually pour in the infused milk, whisking until smooth after each addition. Season to taste and add a pinch of nutmeg.

Bring the sauce to the boil, whisking constantly, then reduce the heat and simmer gently for 5 minutes until smooth and thickened enough to coat the back of a wooden spoon, stirring occasionally. Use as required or transfer to a jug, cover with clingfilm, pressing it into the top of the sauce to prevent a skin forming and leave to cool. Keep in the fridge for up to 2 days.

Madeira Sauce

This has to be one of the nicest sauces that I use in the restaurant and is a vital element of my signature loin of lamb recipe. It also goes very well with beef and chicken. It keeps for up to three days in the fridge if stored in a rigid plastic container or it also freezes well.

Ingredients
(Makes about 200ml (7fl oz))

- 1 tbsp balsamic vinegar
- 1 tbsp soft light brown sugar
- 200ml (7fl oz) Madeira
- 100ml (3 ½fl oz) red wine
- 1 tsp chopped fresh thyme
- 600ml (1 pint) beef stock (see page 214)
- Maldon sea salt and freshly ground black pepper

Method

Pour the balsamic vinegar into a sauce pan and stir the sugar in. Bring to the boil and reduce to simmer on a medium heat for about 2 minutes until reduced to a syrup. Add the Madeira and red wine and return to a simmer for about 6-8 minutes until reduced by half. Add the beef stock and thyme and reduce again for about 20 minutes until thick and glossy and become more concentrated in flavour. Season to taste. Use as required.

Honey and Clove Sauce

If you want to serve this recipe with the duck confit make a double quantity. It keeps for up to a week in a rigid plastic container in the fridge and it is also good with roast pork or even chicken.

Ingredients
(Makes about 200ml (7fl oz))

- 4 tbsp clear honey
- 2 tbsp dark soy sauce
- 2 tbsp balsamic vinegar
- 2 tbsp light muscovado sugar
- 2 tbsp tomato ketchup
- 2 tsp whole cloves
- 225ml (8fl oz) beef stock (see page 214)

Method

Place the honey in a small pan with the soy, vinegar, sugar, ketchup, cloves and stock. Bring to the boil, then reduce the heat and simmer vigorously for 5 minutes or until the mixture has thickened to a sauce consistency which coats the back of a spoon. Season to taste, then pass through a sieve, (discarding the cloves) into a clean pan. Reheat gently and use as required.

Red Onion Marmalade

This onion marmalade can be used in so many different ways and it will keep happily for up to two weeks in the fridge. We get through a lot of it in the restaurant and at home I just love it with cold meats, grilled goat's cheese or in a simple cheese sandwich.

Ingredients
(Makes about 450g (1lb))

- 2 tbsp rapeseed oil
- 5 red onions, thinly sliced
- 1 garlic clove, crushed
- 2 tsp light muscovado sugar
- 200ml (7fl oz) red wine
- 2 tbsp balsamic vinegar
- Maldon sea salt and freshly ground black pepper

Method

Heat the oil in a large pan and cook the onions on a gentle heat for about 10 minutes, stirring occasionally, until softened but not coloured. Stir in the garlic and sugar and then pour in the red wine and balsamic vinegar. Cook gently for about 30-40 minutes until thickened and sticky, stirring occasionally. Season to taste. Store in an airtight container or sterilised jar in the fridge and use as required.

Fig Jam

I normally serve this fig jam with a chicken liver pâté in the restaurant but it is also delicious with goat's cheese or as part of a cheeseboard. I just love the contrast between sweet and savoury and this is something that is well worth having in the fridge, particularly at Christmas time.

Ingredients
(Makes about 900g (2lb))

- 2 tbsp rapeseed oil
- 2 red onions, thinly sliced
- 225g (8oz) ready-to-eat dried figs, finely chopped
- 1 garlic clove, crushed
- 150ml (¼ pint) red wine
- 2 tbsp balsamic vinegar
- 1 tsp caster sugar
- 1 tsp chopped fresh thyme
- Maldon sea salt and freshly ground black pepper

Method

Heat the oil in a large pan and tip in the onions, then cook for 10 minutes until softened but not coloured, stirring occasionally. Stir in figs and garlic until well combined and then pour in the red wine and balsamic vinegar. Cook for about 10 minutes until thickened slightly and the alcohol has cooked off. Stir in the sugar and thyme, then season to taste. Blend in a processor for 1-2 minutes until smooth and leave to cool completely. Store in an airtight container or sterilised jar in the fridge and use as required. This will keep happily for up to two weeks in the fridge.

Apple and Plum Chutney

Apple and plum chutney goes well with pretty much any type of pâté, most cold meats and is also great with cheese. We serve this chutney in the restaurant with our cheese selection but it is also delicious spread thick under some bubbling toasted cheese.

Ingredients
(Makes about 2.65kg (6lb))

- 900g (2lb) plums
- 900g (2lb) apples
- 550ml (17fl oz) cider vinegar
- 450g (1lb) onions, diced
- 450g (1lb) light brown sugar
- 450g (1lb) sultanas
- 1 tsp Maldon sea salt
- 1 tsp ground mixed spice
- 1 tsp ground cloves
- 1 tsp freshly grated root ginger

Method

Halve and core the plums. Peel, core and chop the apples. Put the fruit into a large preserving pan. Then add the cider vinegar, onions, brown sugar, sultanas, salt, spices and ginger. Bring to the boil and gently simmer for one hour until the chutney has nicely reduced and all of the fruit is completely tender. Leave to cool a little and then pack into warm, sterilised jars. Cover with a wax disc and seal when hot. It will store unopened for one year. Once opened, keep it in the fridge and use as required within a couple of weeks.

Port and Balsamic Syrup

This sauce is used daily in the restaurant. I also use it cold but if you want to do this then only simmer for about 10 minutes before allowing to cool completely and chilling down. It will keep in your refrigerator for one month. When you are ready to use it if you find that it has solidified too much either warm it in a small pan or in the microwave, or if you want to use it cold and are finding it is a little thick add a few drops of boiling water to it, stirring to loosen.

Ingredients
(Makes about 200ml (7fl oz))

- 150ml (¼ pint) ruby red port
- 150ml (¼ pint) balsamic vinegar
- 100g (4oz) caster sugar

Method

Place the port in a heavy-based pan with the balsamic vinegar and caster sugar. Bring to the boil, then reduce the heat and simmer for 20 minutes until reduced by one third and the mixture has become thick and syrupy like a honey consistency. Serve at once or allow to cool down completely and store in a bowl covered with clingfilm in the fridge for up to two days. Use as required.

Classic Salad Dressing

To make balsamic dressing, simply replace the red wine vinegar with two tablespoons of balsamic and the sugar with half a teaspoon of honey. Omit the Dijon mustard.

Ingredients
(Makes about 175ml (6fl oz)

- 3 tbsp red wine vinegar
- pinch caster sugar
- 8 tbsp olive or rapeseed oil
- ½ tsp Dijon mustard
- 1 garlic clove, crushed
- Maldon sea salt and freshly ground black pepper

Method

Place the vinegar in a screw-topped jar and add the sugar and a good pinch of salt, then shake until the salt has dissolved.

Add the oil to the jar with the mustard and garlic and shake again until you have formed a thick emulsion. Season to taste and chill until needed.

Five-Spice Balsamic Cream

I tend to use this with seared scallops, roasted duck or as part of a spicy chicken salad but it also works well with pan-fried pork or lamb chops or even steak. Vary the type of stock you use depending on what you are serving it with.

Ingredients
(Makes about 300ml (½ Pint))

- 150ml (¼ pint) beef or chicken stock (page 214 or 215)
- 1 tsp Chinese five-spice powder
- 1 tbsp tomato purée
- 2 tbsp balsamic vinegar
- 150ml (¼ pint) cream
- Maldon sea salt and freshly ground black pepper

Method

Place the stock in a small pan with the five-spice powder, tomato purée, vinegar and cream. Bring to the boil, then reduce the heat and simmer for 20-25 minutes until reduced by a quarter and thickened to a sauce consistency. Season to taste. Use immediately or leave to cool, transfer to a bowl and cover with clingfilm. This can be stored in the fridge for up to three days and reheat as needed.

Mixed Berry Jam

It is a good idea to keep all your jam jars and recycle them. Make sure they are sterilised well, and set aside some time to make your supply of jam. And remember: a pot of jam or chutney is always a welcome gift.

Ingredients
(Makes about 1kg (2¼lb)

- 750g (1½lb) mixed summer berries, including strawberries, raspberries, blueberries and blackberries
- 400g (14oz) caster sugar

Method

Wash and remove any stalks from the fruits. Place in a pan with 100ml (3½fl oz) of water and bring to the boil. Leave to simmer for 10-15 minutes, stirring frequently. Add the sugar, then stir until it has dissolved and boil for a further 15-20 minutes. Transfer to warmed, sterilised jars (a couple of clip jars are perfect) and leave to cool. Once cooled, cover and chill in the fridge where it will thicken and become more jam-like. It will keep for up to two months. Once opened, keep it in the fridge and use as required within a couple of weeks.

Blackcurrant Jam

Lots of people write to me looking for a good jam recipe. I loved blackcurrant jam as a child. My mother always grew her own in her garden, and it is still one of my favourites. So this recipe comes from Vera, my mum.

Ingredients
(Makes about 2.5kg (5lb))

- 1kg bag granulated sugar, still in its packet
- 900g (2lb) blackcurrants, stalks removed
- juice of 1 lemon

Method

Preheat the oven to 100°C (200°F), Gas mark ¼. Warm the sugar in its packet in the very low oven for 30 minutes. Place the blackcurrants in a heavy-based pan with 600ml (1 pint) of water, then bring to the boil and simmer gently until fruit is tender.

Add the warmed sugar to the blackcurrants with the lemon juice. Stir until the sugar is completely dissolved. Bring to the boil again, and boil rapidly for about 20 minutes. Remove from the heat. Have a cold saucer ready, and test by putting a teaspoonful of jam on the saucer. Leave it to cool in the fridge. If the jam wrinkles when you push it with your finger, that means it is ready.

Spoon off any scum from around the edge of the pan, and allow the jam to stand for 15 minutes before stirring once and pouring into warm, sterilised jars. Cover with a wax disc and seal when hot. It will store unopened for one year. Once opened, keep it in the fridge and use as required within a couple of weeks.

Raspberry and Redcurrant Jam

Raspberry and redcurrant jam is another of my favourite jams. I love raspberries and this jam is delicious just spread on your toast. It is also great with scones, served with a good dollop of lightly whipped cream or Irish butter. We serve it in the restaurant at breakfast and also use it regularly in Bakewell tart petit fours.

Ingredients
(Makes about 1.2kg (2½lb))

- 500g (1lb 2oz) granulated sugar, still in the packet
- 500g (1lb 2oz) raspberries
- 200g (7oz) redcurrants, stripped from stalks and then topped and tailed

Method

Preheat the oven to 100°C (200°F), Gas mark ¼. Warm the sugar still in the packet in the very low oven for 30 minutes. Gently crush the fruit and warm it in a pan over a low heat. Then just bring to the boil. Add the warmed sugar, then stir over a low heat until dissolved. Increase the heat and then boil fast for 3-4 minutes. Remove from the heat. Have a cold saucer ready, and test by putting a teaspoonful of jam on the saucer. Leave it to cool in the fridge. If the jam wrinkles when you push it with your finger, that means it is ready.

Spoon off any scum from around the edge of the pan, and allow the jam to stand for 15 minutes before stirring once and pouring into warm, sterilised jars. Cover with a wax disc and seal when hot. It will store unopened for one year. Once opened, keep it in the fridge and use as required within a couple of weeks.

Vegetable Stock

If time allows, I like to leave this vegetable stock to marinate for two days so that the flavours can really infuse and develop. This gives a much fuller taste and is definitely worth the extra wait.

Ingredients
(Makes about 1.2 Litres (2 Pints))

- 2 leeks, trimmed and finely chopped
- 2 onions, peeled and finely chopped
- 2 carrots, peeled and cut into 1cm (½in) dice
- 2 celery sticks, finely chopped
- 1 fennel bulb, cut into 1cm (½in) dice
- 1 head garlic, sliced in half crossways
- 1 fresh thyme sprig
- 1 bay leaf
- 1 tsp pink peppercorns
- 1 tsp coriander seeds
- 1 star anise
- pinch Maldon sea salt

Method

Place all of the ingredients in a large pan and cover with 1.75 litres (3 pints) of cold water. Cover with a lid and bring to a simmer, then remove the lid and cook for another 30 minutes until the vegetables are tender.

Either set aside to marinate for 2 days in a cool place, or if you're short of time, strain through a sieve. Taste – if you find the flavour is not full enough, return to the pan and reduce until you are happy. Use as required or freeze in 600ml (1 pint) cartons or ice cube bags, and defrost when you need it.

Beef Stock

This takes a fair amount of time to make but it is well worthwhile. It is vital to use red wine and tomato purée for real depth of colour. It stores very well in the fridge for three days or can be frozen.

Ingredients
(Makes about 1.7 Litres (3 Pints))

- 675g (1½lb) shin of beef, cut into pieces
- 675g (1½lb) marrow bones or knuckle of veal, chopped
- 1 tbsp rapeseed oil
- 1 onion, peeled and sliced
- 1 carrot, peeled and sliced
- 1 celery stick, sliced
- 1 tbsp tomato purée
- 150ml (¼ pint) red wine
- 1 small garlic bulb, halved
- 1 bouquet garni (parsley stalks, sprigs of thyme and bay leaf tied together)
- ½ tsp salt

Method

Preheat the oven to 220°C (425°F), Gas mark 7. Place the shin of beef and marrow bones or knuckle of veal in a roasting tin and cook in the oven for 30–40 minutes or until well browned. Drain off all the excess oil and discard.

Meanwhile, heat the oil in a large pan. Add the onion, carrot and celery and sauté for about 6-7 minutes until just beginning to colour. Stir in the tomato purée, then pour in the red wine and allow to bubble down for 1 minute.

Add the roasted meat bones to the vegetable and wine mixture with the garlic and bouquet garni. Season with the salt and pour in 1.75 litres (3 pints) of water. Bring to the boil and skim off any scum, then partially cover and reduce the heat to simmer for 4–5 hours until you have achieved a well-flavoured stock, topping up occasionally with a little water, you'll need to add another 1.2 litres (2 pints) in total over the whole cooking time.

Strain the stock and leave to cool completely before chilling down. Once it is cold, remove any trace of solidified fat from the surface using a large spoon, then cover with a lid and return to the fridge until needed. Use as required or freeze in 600ml (1 pint) cartons, and defrost when you need it.

Chicken Stock

I use this chicken stock more than any other type, as it makes the perfect base for soups, stews and sauces. It freezes well so I always have some to hand. I normally make it when we've had a roast chicken for dinner!

Ingredients
(Makes about 1.2 Litres (2 Pints))

- 1 large raw or cooked chicken carcass, skin and fat removed and bones chopped
- 2 leeks, trimmed and chopped
- 2 onions, peeled and chopped
- 2 carrots, peeled and chopped
- 2 celery sticks, chopped
- 1 fresh thyme sprig
- 1 bay leaf
- handful fresh parsley stalks
- 1 tsp white peppercorns

Method

If using a raw chicken carcass, preheat the oven to 180°C (350°F), Gas mark 4 and roast the chicken carcass in a tin for about 40 minutes until golden. Drain through a colander to get rid of excess fat, then chop up.

Place the chopped up chicken carcass in a large pan and cover with 1.8 litres (3 ¼ pints) of cold water. Bring to the boil, then skim off any fat and scum from the surface. Reduce the heat to a simmer and tip in all the remaining ingredients.

Simmer gently for another 1-1½ hours, skimming occasionally and topping up with water as necessary. Taste regularly to check the flavour. When you are happy with it, remove from the heat and pass through a sieve. Leave to cool and remove any fat that settles on the top, then use as required or freeze in 600ml (1 pint) cartons, and defrost when you need it.

Acknowledgements

Over the past three years, I've had the pleasure of developing new and exciting recipes for the Farmers Journal every week. It gives me great satisfaction to know that the recipes are tried, tested and enjoyed in kitchens across Ireland. I'd like to take this opportunity to thank the Farmers Journal readers for their loyalty and support. This book is for all of you!

To all the team in MacNean House and Restaurant - I am so proud of them, and want to thank them for all their hard work and loyalty; Amelda and I are so happy to have them as part of the team and family! A special thank you goes to my head chef Glen Wheeler. I am honoured to have a fantastic support team behind the restaurant. I'd particularly like to thank my business advisor and friend, John Hickey, who is a constant source of direction and inspiration for me.

A big thank you to all the team at the Farmers Journal, especially Mairead Lavery, David Leydon and Ciara O'Kelly. I find their dedication, motivation and creativity to be a constant source of inspiration to me. To all the team associated with bringing my weekly Farmers Journal recipes together - Zara McHugh, Orla Broderick, Sharon Hearne-Smith, John Masterson, Mary Tallent and Jack Caffrey. To the marketing and design team at Márla.ie – Sheila Gallogly, Ann Marie Coonan and Lee Grace. Thanks for another wonderfully designed cookbook!

I'm honoured to have the opportunity to work with so many wonderful people, including David Hare of InProduction, Marty Whelan and Marian Finucane of RTÉ. I would like to thank Bord Bia for their ongoing support; as a Bord Bia ambassador, I am delighted to promote Irish food products at home and abroad.

My work with the Associated Craft Butchers of Ireland has been extremely fulfilling; It is rare to meet people with such vision, passion and knowledge. I look forward to continuing my work with them in the coming years.

And last, but certainly not least, I want to thank my mother Vera, and my wife Amelda, for their continued support during the year, I don't know where I'd be without them!

Neven